Dear Timmy,

Happy birthday!

Think you'll like her;
She digs deep — like
Bondetto.

Hugs! ♡,
Yns

THEATRE AS WITNESS

THREE TESTIMONIAL PLAYS
FROM SOUTH AFRICA

IN COLLABORATION WITH
AND BASED ON THE LIVES OF
THE ORIGINAL PERFORMERS

by Yael Farber

A WOMAN IN WAITING

with Thembi Mtshali-Jones

AMAJUBA: LIKE DOVES WE RISE

with Tshallo Chokwe, Roelf Matlala,
Bongeka Mpongwana, Philip 'Tipo' Tindisa
and Jabulile Tshabalala

HE LEFT QUIETLY

with Duma Kumalo

Foreword by Archbishop Desmond Tutu

Introduction by Amanda Stuart Fisher

Interview between Amanda Stuart Fisher and Yael Farber

OBERON BOOKS
LONDON

First published in 2008 by Oberon Books Ltd
521 Caledonian Road, London N7 9RH
Tel: 020 7607 3637 / Fax: 020 7607 3629
e-mail: info@oberonbooks.com
www.oberonbooks.com

A catalogue record for this book is available from the British Library.

ISBN: 978-1-84002-820-1

Cover design by Dan Steward
Cover photograph of *He Left Quietly* taken by John Hogg
Printed in Great Britain by Antony Rowe Ltd, Chippenham.

CONTENTS

A 16-page plate section can be found

between pages 112 and 113

FOREWORD

by Archbishop Desmond Tutu

Between 1996 and 1999, South Africans across our land gathered in makeshift halls to tell their stories. For many it was the first time they would put words into the world in an attempt to describe indescribable events. Just as important were the witnesses who came to listen…for there is a capacity to heal the human heart in the act not only of speaking – but in finally being heard. Acknowledging the past through sharing one's personal story is the single most powerful action in the battle against the silence of indifference or fear. To testify not only uncovers what lay hidden in a regime's enforced silence – but heals the speaker and the listener alike.

Theatre is the ambitious sister of Testimony. It strives to heal through truth. Yet to tell the same story night after night, as though for the first time, requires great skill and devotion from a performer. Likewise, the structuring of random facts and details into a trajectory from which a powerful theatre experience can emerge, demands much from a playwright and those with whom she is collaborating for a story to be powerfully and truthfully told.

Theatre as Witness is comprised of three testimonial texts – written by Yael Farber in collaboration with the very people who lived these lives as testified, and by whom these stories were originally performed and thus told. These texts are three flames that burn in the darkness of silence and may speak for countless South Africans whose stories will never be told.

A Woman in Waiting, *Amajuba* and *He Left Quietly* have profoundly touched audiences around the world, and as these texts now become accessible, through print, to a greater number of people – one feels the collective dignity of our people rise and make its claim. True story-telling helps us reach beyond the damage, and into the future…to touch every human heart that longs to hear and be heard.

Theatre as Witness continues the trajectory begun by the Truth Commission almost a decade ago, helping us to remember South Africa's past, so that we may forgive but never forget.

It is with great joy that I welcome this remarkable trilogy into the published world.

Archbishop Desmond Tutu

INTRODUCTION

by Amanda Stuart Fisher

The publication of this trilogy of plays by Yael Farber is very timely. At present, both in the UK and beyond, there seems to be an emerging and ever increasing search for the *truth* in stories – both in art and politics. In the political arena, since the fabulated stories of 'weapons of mass destruction' that initiated the invasion of Iraq in 2003, never before have our politicians been regarded with such unprecedented and wide-held distrust. This era of mistrust and its yearning for what is 'true' is illuminated eloquently by playwright, Harold Pinter in his Nobel Lecture (2005):

> '...the majority of politicians, on the evidence available to us, are interested not in truth but in power and in the maintenance of that power. To maintain that power it is essential that people remain in ignorance, that they live in ignorance of the truth, even the truth of their own lives. What surrounds us therefore is a vast tapestry of lies, upon which we feed.'

One of the over-arching concerns of each of the plays in Farber's trilogy is an excavation of the truth; these plays draw out the personal truths of those who lived through the brutality of the Apartheid regime in South Africa and the impoverished socio-economic living conditions endured by the country's indigenous black communities. *Woman in Waiting* tells the story of Thembi Mtshali who as a child was separated from her mother who worked in the kitchens of Durban. Later, as a mother herself, she too is forced to leave her child in order to seek work in the affluent neighbourhood of the white South Africans. In *Amajuba* five actors perform their own stories, providing different personal perspectives on life under the Apartheid regime. Duma Kumalo, one of the Sharpeville Six wrongly accused of murder, is the subject of *He Left Quietly*. In this play Duma Kumalo speaks of his experience of death row and the preparations made for his own death before receiving a last minute reprieve.

Unlike verbatim or documentary theatre, these stories are not drawn from reportage or documentary evidence. Instead Farber harnesses the power of poetry, metaphor and song to craft together theatre texts that bear witness to actual *lived* experience. The authenticity of these stories rests less on their claim to factual veracity, instead it emerges from the 'testimonial truth' of the witness presented before us. Personal testimony of this kind plays a crucial role in the process of history-making because through testimony we can bear witness to what has actually been lived through. The witness, in other words, does not merely add to the weight of factual evidence of what has happened, rather he or she gives voice to that which the objective narrative of history tends to overlook and even suppress. As the theatre director and theorist Rustom Bharucha appositely notes in his paper on South Africa's *Truth and Reconciliation Commission*, the marginalised voice 'has the potential to offer another perspective on dominant narratives, and even to deflect their hegemonic assumptions' (Bharucha in Enwezor, Basualdo, Bauer et al 2002: 362). Testimony is constructed on experiential rather than factual, forensic or historical truths. It is, by its very definition, uniquely personal and subjective. In relation to the facts of an event it might appear fragmentary or insubstantial, because the witness can only testify to their own perception of an event – which is therefore likely to be partial and incomplete. It is a process that is shaped by remembrance, personal feelings and experiences, as Shoshana Felman writes:

> '...testimony seems to be composed of bits and pieces of a memory that has been overwhelmed by occurrences that have not settled into understanding or remembrance, acts that cannot be constructed as knowledge nor assimilated into full cognition.' (Felman and Laub 1992: 5)

Rather than crafting together play texts that *document* the facts of life under the Apartheid regime in South Africa, the voices of the witnesses within these plays enable us to gain access to the experiences and subjectivity of the testimonial subjects with whom Farber has worked. The plays not only bear witness to the plurality of experiences of being black and therefore subject to the harsh laws of Apartheid, but also to the process of remembrance and the painful legacy of this brutal system. Ultimately, the trilogy explores

AMANDA STUART FISHER

the question of moving forward and of reconciling the injustice of the
with the emergent hopes of a new democratic South Africa.

The power of testimony and the process of speaking and listening to each
other as a part of healing, is a concept that permeates throughout Yael
Farber's body of theatrical work. Born in Johannesburg in 1971, Yael Farber
grew up in a South Africa firmly in the grip of Apartheid. Later in the
mid-nineties she watched those who had lived through this unjust regime
relive their experiences on the nightly broadcasts from the *Truth and
Reconciliation Commission* (TRC) as it travelled across South Africa. Farber
belongs to the same generation as the black cast of her play *Amajuba*
and yet as a white South African growing up in the midst of Apartheid
she was painfully aware that her experiences were profoundly different
to those living in neighbouring black townships such as Soweto and
Sharpeville. The numerous Apartheid laws adopted by South Africa's white
government and enforced by the backing of the military and the police
ensured the black people of South Africa were not only kept 'separate'
from their white counterparts but were also condemned to inadequate
housing, little or no education and poor medical and social care. Apartheid
was finally dismantled in the early 1990s and in 1993 the first democratic
elections were held. 1994 saw Nelson Mandela inaugurated as the new
President of South Africa. However, it is evident that the full implications of
the legacy of Apartheid remain as yet unknown, and it is this predicament
that forms the basis of Farber's work: how do the individuals affected by
Apartheid – and ultimately the country itself – try to move forward from
such an unjust history?

In 1995 the *Truth and Reconciliation Commission* was set up 'to help deal
with what happened under Apartheid' (TRC website, 2007). Its aim was to
listen to the testimonies of the victims and the perpetrators of Apartheid in
order to bring about a public and transparent understanding of everything
that had happened. It also had the jurisdiction to make recommendations
to the State President regarding amnesty and reparation. There were and
continue to be many critics of the TRC – particularly around the issue of
reparation and compensation. Yet across the world, the South African TRC
continues to be held in very high regard. This is due perhaps to a shared

admiration of its healing potential. Led by the chairmanship of Archbishop Desmond Tutu, the TRC seemed to create a public space of shared humanity where the pain and suffering of the past could be recounted and listened to. Underpinning the TRC was a constitutional commitment to '*ubuntu*' – an African term which Timothy Murithi describes as 'a cultural world view that tries to capture the essence of what it means to be human' (Murithi 2007). By developing the spirit of *ubuntu* it was hoped the commission would encourage a climate of 'understanding' not 'vengeance'; one of 'reparation' rather than 'retaliation' (TRC 1998). *Ubuntu* encapsulates the notion of *shared* responsibility, as Tutu explains:

> 'It also means that my humanity is caught up, is inextricably bound up, in theirs… We say, 'a person is a person through other people' … I am human because I belong, I participate, I share.' (Tutu in Murithi 2007)

In his forward to the final TRC report published in 1998, Tutu draws attention to the importance of acknowledging the presence of South Africa's past in any conception of a peaceful future. To simply 'forget' the past, he says, would constitute a 'further victimisation of victims by denying their awful experiences' (Tutu in TRC 1998: 7). Tutu unequivocally rejects the possibility of collective 'amnesia' about the atrocities of Apartheid and instead proposes a process of 'calling to account', bringing the brutality of the past and the injustice of Apartheid into the consciousness of everyone. He writes:

> 'The other reason amnesia simply will not do is that the past refuses to lie down quietly. It has an uncanny habit of returning to haunt one. "Those who forget the past are doomed to repeat it" are the words emblazoned at the entrance to the museum in the former concentration camp of Dachau. They are words we would do well to keep ever in mind… We need to know about the past in order to establish a culture of respect for human rights. It is only by accounting for the past that we can become accountable for the future.' (Tutu in TRC 1998: 7)

For Yael Farber, her belief in the healing power of telling one's story is inextricably bound up with the presence of a *listener*. As she indicates in her interview below, it is not only essential for these stories to be told, but

that they must also be listened to and acknowledged. This places
demand on those of us who watch and perform these plays. F(
turn also bear witness to the testimonies that emerge from these t...
demand is an ethical one and calls into question the issue of responsibility.
The problem of being a spectator to someone else's pain and suffering is
articulated succinctly by Rustom Bharcuha who asks:

> 'What happens when you are not a victim yourself, but you become a
> spectator of someone else's pain? How do you deal with it? How do you
> resist the obvious possibilities of voyeurism, or the mere consumption
> of other people's suffering? How do you sensitise yourself politically
> to the histories of others that might not have touched on your own?'
> (Bharucha in Enwezor, Basualdo, Bauer et al 2002: 397)

In order to think through these questions further, it is useful to consider
the basis of Farber's methodology – in particular the creative relationship
forged with the individuals whose stories are explored in the plays. It is,
in fact, the *quality* of these relationships that safeguards the integrity
of the work. In each case, the testifying subject was not only intimately
involved with the development of the piece but also performed their
testimonial story as well. As is evident from the interview with Farber, these
collaborative relationships were constructed on trust, respect and through
developing dialogue.

The potency of Farber's approach is that whilst the stories speak to us
of the specificities of the unjust Apartheid regime, the heart of the work
transcends this historical moment. The characters in these plays also
engage with central questions that concern us all: what does it mean to be
human? Is it possible to overcome the trauma and melancholia of the past
and forge a new future?

In each of these plays the characters seem to occupy a position that is
suspended between the past and the future of South Africa. These
characters not only speak of past injury, their presence in the text, their
bodies and their voices attest to the challenge of moving forward from the
past to the future.

Written in collaboration with Thembi Mtshali, *Woman in Waiting* was Farber's first testimonial play. It is an evocative and powerful piece that explores Mtshali's life as a young child waiting for months at a time for her mother to return from the city where she had gone to work. Later, as a mother herself caring for the children of white families in the city, she again has to wait each week to be allowed to return to her own baby whom she was forced to leave to be 'breastfed by her sister'. Thembi's story testifies to her personal strength and, in common with the other two plays in the trilogy, *Woman in Waiting* bears witness to the triumph of the individual human spirit over the adversity and political brutality of the Apartheid system. Through their brave and painful confrontations with the past, the testifying subjects within each of these plays raise important questions about personal agency, empowerment and the challenges of forging a new future for themselves and South Africa. This is articulated by Mtshali when, near the end of *Woman in Waiting*, she speaks of the fragile connections between the past and the future and the importance of confronting what has gone before, saying: '*When I walk through this museum in me, I understand the power of facing the past.*' Of course, Mtshali's story also bears witness to the difficulty of reconciling what has been lived through with the possibilities offered by the new South Africa. For whilst the future promises a better life for black South Africans, the Apartheid regime left a concrete and brutal legacy in the form of permanent physical and psychological damage inflicted on those who were subject to its unjust laws and systems. An unbearable sense of mourning and loss resonates throughout Thembi's words. So, when she speaks to her child of what is lost to the past, she says:

> 'There is time lost that I mourn. Time I can never reclaim… If I had the power – I would trade the moments I walked someone else's child in the park, while you took your first steps on this earth – and I was not there to throw you up in the air and call you a Queen. But it is gone this time, and I can never trade it back.' (page 73)

The possibility of moving forward into the future and the challenges this brings is a central theme in *Amajuba* – the second in this trilogy and again written in collaboration with the five actors who performed it. What is striking in *Amajuba* is the sheer diversity of experiences that are presented in the play. Through the stories of Bongi, Jabu, Tipo, Roelf and Tshallo we encounter the many different faces of Apartheid. Through their testimonial stories we learn of the physical and psychological impacts of this regime, gaining insight into how Apartheid inexorably shaped their formative experiences and ultimately their very subjectivity. Through the use of vernacular languages, the text captures the plurality of truths and experiences at play in any story of South Africa. This approach draws attention to the politics and violence of language itself. For the subjectivity of the characters in *Amajuba* is framed by the sovereignty of the languages they speak. They have grown up with the knowledge that the language of their home and heritage has no place in the public sphere of 'White South Africa'. As Farber indicates in her interview, when the characters speak to us in English they are not speaking to us in their first language. Consequently, when vernacular languages are adopted to narrate the past, what is opened up is the possibility of reclaiming, in a profound sense, the cultural identity that was historically suppressed by the governing laws and systems of Apartheid. The stories, indigenous songs and languages bear witness to this and to a historical process that forced the black majority to live as outsiders in their own land.

He Left Quietly, written in collaboration with Duma Kumalo, is the third play in this trilogy. The story of the Sharpeville Six received international attention in the early eighties: it seemed to finally rouse the world's conscience to the violence and illegitimacy of South Africa's Apartheid regime. Yet in *He Left Quietly* Farber directs our attention away from the politics of the situation and instead explores the existential trauma of Kumalo himself. The result is an extraordinary play that engages with Duma Kumalo's traumatic confrontation with death and his reflections on what it means to be human. Duma's experience on death row, the lack of humanity within the Apartheid justice system and his observations of the easy *disposability* of life seems to awaken in him an existential understanding of the finitude of life itself.

By drawing attention to those who did not survive, whose stories will never be told, Kumalo bears witness on behalf of the other. Through his testimony he reflects on the end of his innocence and the disappearance of his previous 'self'. He realises that not only has his past existence been shattered but that his future has been irretrievably shaped by the brutality and injustice of what happened. He will never be the same man he was when he left home to join the protest in Sharpeville; his fate is inexorably bound to the trauma of death row. He says:

'I have never really come home.
One thing is certain that I didn't know.
Every night, I am back there.
Every night – I go home to Death Row.' (page 205)

Duma Kumalo personifies the double imperative of bearing witness: the desire to tell one's own story and the need to speak for others, for those who did not survive. The paradox of this imperative is that whilst the testimony of the witness is utterly personal, the compulsion to speak is prompted by a need to bear witness on behalf of those who did not survive and therefore can not speak. This vital need to speak and to communicate what happened to the rest of the world, is acknowledged by Auschwitz survivor, Primo Levi, who says:

'The need to tell our story to "the rest", to make "the rest" participate in it, had taken on for us, before our liberation and after, the character of an immediate and violent impulse, to the point of competing with our other elementary needs.' (Levi 1979: 15)

It is here, in Levi's words, that we begin to glimpse the 'ethical demand' that is issued by the performance of testimony. This demand speaks to the listener and asks us to consider how we participate in the story that is being told to us. What is our responsibility to the witness who speaks before us?

If we consider the notion of *ubuntu* we can begin perhaps to see how interconnected our histories really are. Once we have heard these testimonies, we cannot 'unhear' them. To turn away from these stories is to deny the humanity of those who have suffered and who are telling us their story. The responsibility of listening to these testimonies raises some important questions: What is the substance of the ethical demand that is being issued in the telling of these stories? What does it mean for us, in terms of our shared responsibility, as readers, audience members, performers?

For Duma Kumalo, his seemingly haphazard decision to join the protest changed his past and his future irrevocably. The experience seems to have politicised him. Near the end of the play he speaks of the importance of shared responsibility and the need to align oneself with one's history, to participate and to stand up and take part. He says:

'This is our history. We all come from this broken place.
Either you are in or you are out. But if you choose to be in – you must partake.' (page 234)

BIBLIOGRAPHY

Enwezor, O., Basualso, C., Bauer, U. et al (2002) *Experiments with Truth: Documenta 11_Platform 2 Germany*, Hatje Cantz Publishers.

Felman, S. and Laub, D.(1992) *Testimony: Crises of Witnessing in Literature, Psychoanalysis, and History,* Abingdon, Routledge.

Levi, P. 1987 *If This is a Man. The Truce,* London, Abacus Press.

Murithi, T. (2007) *Practical Peacemaking Wisdom from Africa: Reflections on Ubuntu*, University of Bath website (http://people.bath.ac.uk/edsajw/monday/Ubuntu.htm August 1st 2007).

Pinter, H. (2005) Nobel Lecture: Art, Truth & Politics, Nobel Prize website (http://nobelprize.org/nobel_prizes/literature/laureates/2005/pinter-lecture.html November 1st 2007)

Truth and Reconciliation Commission of South Africa Report, Vol 1, Chapter 1, 2003, South African Government Information website (www.infor.gov.za/otherdocs/2003/trc)

Interview between Amanda Stuart Fisher and Yael Farber

ASF: You've described the plays in this volume as 'testimonial', can you tell us what you mean by your use of the term?

YF: To me 'testimonial theatre' is a genre wrought from people bearing witness to their own stories through remembrance and words. Material culled from memory is crafted into a compelling yet true narrative, which is then brought to life through text, performance and the visual devices of theatre. The essential component of this genre lies in its capacity for healing through speaking, hearing and being heard.

ASF: Could you tell us about your creative process?

YF: Memory is seldom effortlessly accessible, linear, comprehensive or even necessarily compelling when told. In my experience, an individual's story will first emerge in a very two-dimensional narrative, driven by dates and dry accounts of watershed moments.

My first step is to let the subject expel the narrative in this way in order to map out the exploration ahead – like the markings an archaeologist makes in the dust before beginning the dig. I then proceed by asking specific but simple questions: 'A Christmas day from childhood – what was the colour of your dress? What did your shoes look like?' The real story will inevitably emerge in the delicate human details. As an example, when we were creating *A Woman in Waiting*, Thembi Mtshali-Jones responded: 'Well actually my shoes were always too small, because my mother could only come once a year to visit me. She would measure my feet with a piece of string and then the following Christmas she always arrived with shoes that would have fitted my feet the year before!' This made the two of us laugh – but at the same time, I found this to be a very poignant symbol of missing out on a year of the growth of your child. It's a detail that would not have emerged if I'd asked someone to simply tell me about their life. I make extensive notes during this process, but I take care not to make the subject aware of the power of the emerging metaphors. When gathering material, the person telling their story should not be consciously looking to contrive a compelling narrative. It is *my* responsibility to be holding the larger frame. The survivor needs to be liberated to access random, chaotic raw memory. It is an entirely organic process dictated in the moment, by what I sense we need to do to keep going deeper. The cast spends this period of creation in intensive interviews with me; singing childhood songs; writing letters to family members to say the unspoken; telling me their dreams in the mornings...

ASF: The dreams they are having while they are creating the play?

YF: Right. So each morning we meet and the first thing we speak about is: 'What did you dream last night?' During the unearthing process, dreams are usually rampant. The subconscious sifts and processes issues in a profoundly image-based, theatrical way that offers rich possibilities. There is little respite from the intensity of this exploration. I have never had more than six weeks in which to create a new work, starting from scratch to opening night. So the gathering of material; the writing and shaping it into text; and then staging and rehearsal of the work has to happen concurrently. About two weeks into the process of gathering raw material – I must therefore already begin shaping it. I do this in the evenings, away from the cast. I write at night – usually through the nights, due to the time limitations. Despite being based on true events – testimony does not come with a natural dramatic arc. This must be worked and paced. The audience needs to be transported from indifference to empathy, from their own limited perspective to deep inside the interior landscape of another person's world. I am constantly on the lookout for the detail that an audience will recognise in their own lives in order to bridge them into a life so dramatically different from their own. For example, the listener may not relate to becoming a freedom fighter at fifteen years old as Tshallo Chokwe in *Amajuba* did. But one *can* relate to being afraid of the dark as a child – so this is how we began his narrative. The barriers we construct to differentiate ourselves from one another, collapse under the weight of the evidence that we all inevitably share these fragile 'once-upon-a times'. So, I spend the night hours structuring such narrative, scripting dialogue and monologues; working to ensure the story is cohesive and moving, while remaining true to the subjects' life events. The very dense file of material accumulating day by day must be shaped into a trajectory which fits the limited time frame of a theatre piece. I usually end up only using about ten percent of what I have gathered, and the subjects certainly don't tell me anywhere near a quarter of their lives. It all comes down to the editing of this material, deciding what to include and then shaping and scripting these events into a piece of theatre. Each morning, I return to the company with pages of new text which the cast will read and 'try on'. Dialogue is translated by the cast into vernacular, and speech patterns and vocabulary are touched if needed – to retain an integrity and authenticity particular to each performer. Afternoon sessions are spent staging the emerging scenes – a process which inevitably brings additional depth and texture to the development. We collaboratively layer the work in this way. From there, my work as a director begins. This is a whole new phase of the process that is critical to how the work is pitched – avoiding sensationalism and indulgence, while doing justice to the pains of the past through deeply authentic performances in a simple but powerful piece of theatre.

ASF: How do you actually encourage the individuals you work with to stay the course in this process?

YF: Each actor has to be approached so differently. One has to be intuitive in how to go about accessing the material needed. At times it can feel like quite an aggressive process.

The person you're working with may feel invaded – perhaps even brutalised by the experience, because the memories they are recovering *are* brutal. What I've found to be very helpful is to constantly remind the actor that if these memories were easy, they wouldn't be important. We talk a lot as a company about how it may be difficult to tell these stories but it's not going to be easy for the audience to hear these stories either, and that they potentially offer a transformative power for all. I do believe in the ancient concept that the actor has a calling to channel the needed catharsis of their community. The audience benefits from this in the safety and privacy of the dark auditorium, while the actors – those especially brave, dangerous souls – choose to go out and strip their skins away each night, and express the collective truth for us all.

ASF: How would you classify your work, do you see it as political?

YF: I prefer 'human' as opposed to 'political' – but clearly it *is* political. The work brings news of lives that are profoundly impacted upon by a socio-political system – but through human detail rather than political rhetoric. Tell people a good story and they will inevitably imbibe the politics of context. But political rhetoric does not theatre make! I specifically avoid using phrases, terms and words that are over-identified with an issue. We are in the business of telling stories – and this can only be achieved through delicate human detail.

ASF: Can these plays be performed by other people?

YF: These narratives have been wrought from real experiences but should not remain limited to being performed by the original casts. The possibility of other actors carrying these testimonies forward offers a life force for stories that should continue to be heard. What is important in testimonial theatre, however, is that the audience is clear on whether the storyteller is an actor honouring another person's story – or if the narrator is the person who actually lived these events. We were preparing

YAEL FARBER / AMANDA STUART FISHER

Amajuba for a tour, and once found ourselves an actor down at the very last minute. I urgently had to cast Bongi Mpongwana as a replacement to narrate the existing story of the missing actor as if it were her own. But the integrity of the production immediately felt compromised. This wasn't because she was not telling her own story – but rather because she would be the *only one* pretending, while the other four storytellers had lived the events they were telling. This becomes confusing for an audience. You are cutting a deal with your audience about how far to suspend their disbelief. If they are moved but this deal is unclear – they will feel manipulated, duped. Be clear with your listeners and the integrity of the experience remains intact. Bongi has such an extraordinary past of her own, that – in any case – there was no way I could ask her to go on stage and pretend to have lived someone else's life events when the platform was there to tell her own. So we worked round the clock for five days and re-wrote the material in time for the tour, to depict her experiences as the new fifth testimony in the show. This set the precedent.

ASF: What inspires you to work this way?

YF: As a South African artist, I wanted to be a part of revealing how individual lives were violated by Apartheid – as well as documenting these stories in a way that history text books cannot convey. Not only is it an issue of revealing the past, but remembering and acknowledging this past to the new generations through testimony, using the power of theatre. There is also something very profound about working to reclaim this past. I have found that through the creative process, there is a growing sense of *value* from the subject *towards* their own story. In South Africa, suffering is so intrinsically a part of the black experience that initially when the actors were asked to delve into their past, there was a certain embarrassment. They were self-consciousness about why their story, above anyone else's, would be important enough to be told. I think that's very symptomatic of a traumatised community. No one feels they have the right to take the floor, because why should they and not other more 'significant' stories be heard? Being an outsider as director and scripter, it is a continual necessity to reassure the person whose story it is – that their story will represent the many that will remain *untold*.

ASF: In *A Woman in Waiting* there's a very powerful line in the text, when Thembi says: 'When I walk through this museum in me I understand the power of facing the past'. How do you think that your work contributes to the process of moving forward from the Apartheid years in South Africa?

YF: Put very simply, I profoundly believe that speaking is a form of healing. Until you've told your story – even if you intellectually understand you have been wronged – the memories may remain a source of secrecy, pain or shame. Speaking and being heard is a modest but profound beginning. The shattered history of South Africa will take generations to heal, but I believe theatre has a significant role in this process. The power of having a *listener*, was evident during the *Truth and Reconciliation Commission*. It was at least a platform for survivors to finally *speak* and have people *bear witness to their pain*. Without a listener who believes and empathises with you, you are dislocated from – yet deeply shaped by – your own story. To own the events of one's life and share these memories is to reclaim one's self and offer your community, your witnesses a collective possibility to do the same. I have no illusions of permanently eradicating severe trauma through this process. To harbour such expectations would be irresponsible both to the individuals who have entrusted me with their stories, as well as to the very piece of theatre we are trying to create. To be lost in self-important notions of being healers would be deluded and result in some very indulgent work. We are storytellers. Our task is simply to tell a story well. But I do know that if we get it right, there can be a tremendous healing power that results from speaking, listening and being heard.

YAEL FARBER / AMANDA STUART FISHER

ASF: So thinking about that, how do you negotiate the creative ownership of the work? I mean are there ever any disagreements about what should or shouldn't be used?

YF: There are always moments when an actor will say 'I'd be really uncomfortable if that was exposed'. But I've found that if you can enter into a dialogue of integrity with the actor, they begin to understand how profoundly important it is that they break the silence on precisely the details that cause shame or secrecy. Shame is usually a heat-seeking missile for precisely what is most valuable for the narrator to expose and publicly claim.

ASF: Can I ask you now about the use of the different languages in the plays?

YF: Telling a story to reclaim yourself, in a language that has been enforced on you by a dominating regime, is a contradiction in itself. However, language is your bridge to reach out to the wider community of the world…or the perpetrator, who will very often not speak the survivor's mother tongue. Language – as in any occupied, colonised land – is such a hot, delicate issue in South Africa. When the nationalist government came into power in the '40s, education was divided into Christian National Education for white children and what was called Bantu Education for black children. One education was completely designed towards servitude and the other towards being the master. If you were black, you could not be educated in your first language. The Soweto uprising of 1976 was triggered by a new law declaring that all subjects would now be taught in Afrikaans in the townships, which was the language of the Nationalist government. Even as a white schoolchild – if I had been told that I had to take all my lessons in Afrikaans, I would not have graduated from high school. It was a guaranteed method of educationally crippling generations of black students.

There's a fundamental connection between the psyche of the country and the languages that people speak. The denigrating of indigenous language through colonialism is a psychic violence.

It was central to these three plays that authentic indigenous language be intrinsic to the texts. When the actor speaks in their vernacular, the actor is deep in their integrity, while the audience is momentarily an 'outsider' who misses out. When the actor then breaks from vernacular, and returns to English – the audience no longer takes this for granted, but is aware that this storyteller is reaching out in a language imposed upon them – which is a profoundly generous act.

ASF: Moving on to your third play, *He Left Quietly* which stylistically seems to develop a different direction to the other plays. Could you tell us a little bit about this?

YF: Well, as a theatre maker you have to be a pragmatist! I would have loved it if Duma could've done a one-man show, but it was clear to me that he needed to be afforded the solace and dignity of sitting in a chair and telling his story from a place of stillness. But how then to capture the chaos of the events? Creative decisions emerge from very practical problems! I decided I was going to get an actor to represent Duma as a young man – his split-off self caught in the past, while an older wiser Duma reflected and looked on. That meant Duma was not slave to some kind of frenetic pace – which he wasn't in physical shape for anyway. Furthermore I felt this device would bring a certain kind of abstraction, a cooling to the re-enactment in order to ensure the audience's stamina and reduce sensationalism when depicting such catastrophic events.

ASF: When we were talking earlier, you said that Duma had said to you that even his story wasn't his own. Could you say a little bit about what you think he meant by this?

YF: Duma Kumalo was an extraordinary man who survived Death Row with his humanity somehow in tact. He passed away last year and I am currently writing his biography. For the title of the biography I've used a phrase that he once said to me, which took me to the core of his interior moral world: We were sitting and talking late one night and I, grappling with how he had remained or become the man he was, asked, "But is not your most burning question: 'Why me? Why did this have to happen to me?'" He just looked at me and said: 'If not me, who?'

Over the years we developed a long conversation about that. His response to his story was always: it *happened* to him but he didn't *architect* it. It was a strange tangled web of events that he got caught in, but this story didn't *belong* to him. It *belonged* to the random nature of that time and the larger picture of its context. It ultimately comes back to the notion of: 'There but for the grace of God go I'. And that's what Duma always encapsulated – even when he spoke about his perpetrators. When I asked him: 'How do you feel about the prosecutor who so viciously pursued your death sentence?' Duma simply said 'Oh, he was a young man and I think he was after his promotion'. For Duma, none of us own our stories – they just happen through us. He refused to claim some kind of ownership of his story. He believed it belonged to the world that had shaped it – in all its evil and all its redemptive possibilities. There were people around him who were very possessive about who had first heard his story and who had the right to be involved in the telling of that story. I understand that. As artists, I think, we tend to try to colonise a story. As a creator, one must face that part of oneself that has over-identified with the work and feels possessive over the subject. When someone like Duma, who lived and nearly died his story, insists: 'This doesn't belong to me, this is just what happened to me and I must work with anyone who will help me bring news of what I lived' – it is profoundly humbling. You understand that you too are just part of the channel through which this story – these stories – must be told.

ASF: Could you say something about how the work has been received in South Africa?

YF: We've only had very limited runs in South Africa due to the desperate lack of funding for theatre at home. Ironically it has

en far easier to have international presenters pick up the
works than it has been to get South African producers interested.
But when we have had the privilege of playing to audiences at
home, responses have been very intense and emotional. One of
the extraordinary things South African audiences – particularly
black audience members – tend to do is, at the most brutal
and savage moments of a story – they laugh! This is obviously
very disconcerting for people in the audience who don't share
this reaction. But in South Africa you come to understand this
laughter. It's a laughter of recognition, of survival – a laughter
of somebody tapping into the secrets of the community. It is
an extended shattered kind of cry. I've watched particularly
older people in the audiences whose lives were destroyed by
Apartheid – laughing so much that they are wiping tears from
their eyes, shoulders shaking, giggling behind hankies. Laughter
comes from the centre of our humanity and pain. It is the sound
that manifests when we know we are witnessing the truth.

A WOMAN IN WAITING

Created & written by Yael Farber
With Thembi Mtshali-Jones

A HISTORY OF TEXT AND PRODUCTION DEVELOPMENT

Born in 1957, Thembi Mtshali-Jones has lived most of her life in Apartheid South Africa's iron hold. Her life journey has led her from a childhood of poverty in the rural village of Sabhoza; to the urban township of Kwamashu and the white suburbs of Durban – where she found employment as a domestic worker and child care-giver; to Johannesburg, she would, over the years, become one of South Africa's foremost performers and singers. In 1999, during a three year stay in Washington DC, she received a late-night call from Yael Farber who was in New York for several months directing a production.

For Farber, a new creation always begins with a single image. Riding a train early one morning into New York, she had seen a dress hanging on a washing line, drifting in half circles in the morning breeze. This limp, worn-out garment looked – for a poignant moment – like a tired woman washed, wrung and hung out to dry. There was a spent yet attendant quality to the posture of the dress suspended from the line that put Farber in mind of the stoic patience she had noticed in the humble women of the country she grew up in. This state of profound patience was embodied particularly by the women who had attended the Truth and Reconciliation Hearings in South Africa. Come to hear, finally, what had happened to their 'disappeared' loved ones decades earlier – these women seemed, to Farber, to reflect a spiritual triumph over the deep powerlessness wrought by the ineptitudes and indignities that Apartheid had imposed. Farber had been pondering a new creation that morning on the train to New York, a work that would convey the extraordinary struggle and courage of black women in South Africa in the face of such hardship. The lone dress drifting on a washing line germinated the seed that was to become *A Woman in Waiting*.

The call to Thembi Mtshali-Jones was timely. After a long and successful career in South Africa, Mtshali-Jones was longing to perform biographical material close to her heart. Years previously, she had been inspired by renowned South African theatre maker Barney Simon who had worked with her in creating songs based on her rural childhood and experience as a domestic worker. For some time, she had wanted to tell her own story of life lived as a black woman in the country of her birth. She agreed to come to New York immediately to begin work.

Farber approached the Africa Exchange Foundation – an international program of 651 Arts in New York City – for support of the project. The Joseph Papp Public Theater's resident dramaturge of that time, John Diaz, met with Farber, agreeing to host the project at The Joseph Papp Public Theater, if financially supported by 651 Arts. Though there was still much redtape to get through before funding could be confirmed, Mtshali-Jones and Farber were determined to begin the process.

With less than $10 between them, no road map and minimal experience in right-hand driving – the two women brazenly set out in a borrowed car for a house in Vermont – generously offered by friends Amy Redford and Lola Van Wagenen, as a retreat in which to work. During this time of solitude, Farber interviewed Mtshali-Jones extensively. This was a painful process of excavating the past. Besieged by childhood memories, Mtshali-Jones unearthed deeply personal material which was then structured and scripted into a text by Farber during this time. The two women returned to New York several weeks later. With Farber continuing the writing process through the nights, and the two women rehearsing and adjusting the material during the day, A Woman in Waiting began to emerge. Hours before flying back to Johannesburg, the work was showcased to the Public Theater staff and George C. Wolfe, and invited to return for further development.

A Woman in Waiting opened to great success at the National Arts Festival back in Grahamstown, South Africa in 1999. In the years that followed, the production has played to critical acclaim in South Africa; North Africa (winning the Carthage Festival Best Performance award); the USA and at the Edinburgh Festival (where the production was received with a stunning response from audience and critics alike, winning a prestigious Scotsman Fringe First Award in its first week of performance and playing to sold out houses).

An extensive tour of the United Kingdom, produced by UK Arts International, followed – transferring to London's West End in 2001. The radio version of *A Woman in Waiting*, recorded by the BBC, was awarded the prestigious Gold Sony Award for Best Drama. Tours to the USA, Canada and Bermuda followed. The work continues to travel under the management of The Farber Foundry.

It was whilst watching the televised Truth and Reconciliation Hearings each Sunday night several years ago that I was first struck by a haunting, silent presence on the periphery of these proceedings: the women – mothers, daughters, wives of those murdered or still missing – who had come to the hearings finally to learn the truth about the deaths of their loved ones. The patience and forbearance of these women struck a deep chord. They seemed to have the waiting thread knitted inextricably into the fabric of their souls.

Where had these women learned such grace and dignity in the face of South Africa's darkness and personal despair?

This unique state of waiting is so familiar to those who have grown up in this troubled country. We have witnessed – indeed come to expect – such stoicism from the silent force of women here: queuing endlessly for transport every morning and evening, waiting silently to clear employers' dinner tables, calmly waiting to see their children once a year at Christmas time.

These matriarchs are the spine of a society that has endured the limit a regime can impose. Women have always been the filters for a society: the vessels through which the pain of a community flows. Whether or not we choose to acknowledge the pain of our past, it is a tangible force that waits – like these women – for its time to be acknowledged.

A Woman in Waiting is a celebration of one such woman.

Thembi Mtshali-Jones – like most South African women – has a story of waiting to tell. She shared her story with me with courage and honesty – and from her life events we have created a piece of theatre which we hope may speak for those who never will.

Yael Farber
Grahamstown, South Africa, 1999

A WOMAN IN WAITING

Based on the life of Thembi Mtshali-Jones

This work should ideally be played on the floor to a raked audience – as opposed to on a raised stage – so that contact with the audience is immediate and dynamic. As the audience enters, the stage is bare but for a large wooden crate standing centre stage. Props are kept to a minimum. The actress never leaves the stage once the performance begins.

A Woman in Waiting *runs without an interval.*

ONE • COUNTING FULL MOONS

(*A woman is singing in the dark. Lights rise slowly on a large, roughly hewn wooden crate lying on its side. The lid is open to lie flat on the floor. As lights grow, we see the woman is inside the crate, on her back. She moves her arms and legs slowly and sensuously – as though suspended in water. The musical phrase she sings is filled with longing, and will be repeated at certain junctures during the show. She sits up slowly and looks out at the audience from the confines of this box.*)

THEMBI   Izulu laliduma – ligqazuluka, libanika, isiphepho siwisa izihlahla imifula Igcwele ichichima.

[There was a great thunderstorm – lightning was cutting through the trees that were falling from a heavy gale and the rivers were full and overflowing with water.]

It was the day the heavy rains came – and the wind was blowing so hard, that when my mother came to cross Umkhumbane River to go to the hospital, she knew she would drown if she stepped into the water.

And so she waited…

(*Curling up into a foetal position.*)

CHILD IN WOMB   Tswee Tswee! [The sound of a small chick]
Seng'vuthiwe! [I'm cooked!]
I'm cooked. I'm ready.

THEMBI   (*Smiling at the memory.*)
Perhaps I should've been a little more patient, and waited for the river to catch its breath. But this was before I had seen the world beyond my mother's womb: a world that would teach me to wait…

And yet unborn and fearless, I saw no point in waiting for a better time to arrive.

CHILD IN WOMB (*Desperately.*)
Tswee Tswee! Seng'vuthiwe! [I'm cooked!]
I'm cooked! I'm ready!

THEMBI (*Leaping from the box.*)
…And tumbled into my mother's arms.

(*Switching effortlessly into the roles of her* MAMA *and* FATHER *respectively.*)

MAMA (*Holding an imaginary baby girl in her arms.*)
Baba, intombazane. Igama lakhe uThembekile.

[Baba, (a term of respect used when addressing an older man) it's a girl. Her name is Thembekile.]

Her name is Thembekile.

Thembi [abbreviated form of Thembekile] Mtshali!

THEMBI My father gave me the praises of our Ancestors.

FATHER (*In the traditional rhythmic style of praising.*)
You are the child of amaMtshali.

OHlabangane – Magalela, agase njengengonyama.

[Son of Hlabangane – who was a son of Magalela, the one who attacks like a lion!]

Mantshinga, ovutshwe ngamasi asechobeni khondlo.

[Who was the son of Mantshinga, the great warrior –]

Hlangabeza – Mlambo ka Nyathi.

[Who was the son of Hlangabeza – who was the son of Mlambo – who was the son of Nyathi.]

This is where we come from! And this is who you are!

MAMA   (*With great deference to her husband.*)
        Baba [father – term of respect, rather than literally one's father], what about her Christian name?
        You know the world will demand it.

FATHER   (*Thrown by the request, but trying to hold his authority.*)
         Er…yes – ah – Rose? …um… Pinky? Gloria? Beauty!

THEMBI   But as the wind continued to roar its praises…

FATHER   (*Suddenly illuminated.*) Aha! Heavygale!

         Ja! [Yes!] Thembekile Heavygale Mtshali!

THEMBI   (*In dismay.*)
         Heavygale! HEAVYGALE! I always hated the sound of it.

         It was like I was to blame for something…

         Like I had brought the passion of the weather from another world.

         I thought *that* was the reason my parents sent me to Zululand to live with my grandparents in the village of Sabhoza. But Gogo [Granny], my grandmother, explained to me:

GRANNY   Mntanomtanami [Grandchild], don't cry. Your mama is working in the 'Kitchens' [White Suburbs] in Durban. But me and Mkhulu [Grandfather], your Grandfather will take care of you. Your mama will come for you when the time is right.

Mntanomtanami you must wait...

(*THEMBI sings the opening theme softly, and sits on the open lid of the box on the floor, looking up at the sky.*)

THEMBI   When I was a little girl, my best friends were the birds. They had the freedom of flying anywhere they wished, and I would give them secret messages to take to my parents in Durban.

(*She sings.*)

Wen'usematholeni, *
[Out there in the fields,]
Ijuba ijahelikhulu.
[The doves are everywhere.]

(*As a small girl of approximately six years old, she watches the sky anxiously – waiting for the Ncede Bird to appear. She sees him suddenly in a nearby tree.*

In the below speech, the words in italics indicate that the letter R is, at times, pronounced as an L – a linguistic trait of rural Zulu speakers.)

CHILD THEMBI   Hei Ncede! I've been waiting for you under this tree for de whollo [whole] day. I have a *velly* [very] important message for you to take to Mama and Baba in Durban.

Tell them my arm...she's nearly long enough to touch my ear – so I can start school!

Mama says that when I finish small school here, I will come and live with her in Durban, because the big school is far away!

---

* Lyrics extracted from song taught to Thembi by her grandmother in Sabhoza Village. Original source is unknown.

Tell Mama I am waiting for my *Chlismas* [Christmas] clothes and new shoes. Hey Ncede – this is *velly* important!

Tell them that my feet *glow* [grow] during the year.

They don't stay the same size as when they measured them with a *stling* [string] last *Chlismas*.

They always forget that. OK, hamba manje! [OK, go now!]

I will wait for you here. *Tomollow* [tomorrow] and *tomollow* and the other *tomollow*…

(She watches with great longing – as the bird flies away. She sings.)

Khele Khele Nkoviyo! / Uphetheni ngomlomo?*

[Hey there big owl! / What are you carrying with your mouth?]

Ngipheth'amas'omtwana. / Uwasaphi na?

[I'm carrying my baby's food. / Where are you taking it?]

Ngiwasa kozong'nceda! / Ancedeni na?

[To someone who will help me! / Help you with what?]

Athi qgi qgi qgi! / Ame ngeguma lakwa mnewabo.

[To run faster / Wait next to my brother's house.]

Ath'umnewabo ngena laph'endlini / Ngiyabe ngiyangene.

[My brother will let me in / When I'm inside.]

Ngafica izajeje! / Ngezani naphela? / Ngezabayeni

[There's lots of food! / What is it for? / It's for the in-laws]

Bafik'enini? / Bafik'izolo. / Wabahlabisani?

[When did they come? / They came yesterday / What did you slaughter?]

* Lyrics extracted from song taught to Thembi by her grandmother in Sabhoza Village. Original source is unknown.

Ngabahlabis' ucilo. / Kodwa ucilo bayamala!

[A small animal / The in-laws refused it]

Baqond'imvubu! / Yona nyam'enkulu!

[They want a big animal! / A hippopotamus!]

Badle baphelele nezithembu zabo.

[That they can all eat with their families.]

Wo-yeye, ha-wu! Wo-yeye!

THEMBI   (*Turning to the audience.*)

Could someone explain this thing called 'time' to me? Is the moon moving faster these days than it used to? Why do I feel like just as they're taking the Christmas decorations down in the shopping malls...before I've turned around...they're putting them back up again.

And that Boney M... (*Singing the title.*) 'By the Rivers of Babylon' is back again.

But when I was a child, a year took twelve full moons to pass!

(*She counts each moon on her ten fingers and two toes.*)

And many more moons for your arm to grow long enough... (*Reaching over her head to touch the opposite ear.*) ...to touch your ear...

So that you can start school!

(*She climbs onto the wooden crate, and dangles her legs like a small child.*)

CHILD THEMBI   Jack and Jill went up the hill...
(*Mangling the words of the English nursery rhyme.*)
To fitch-a-pala-wata! Jack fell down...
(*Lost in the incomprehensible rhyme.*)
Um – ah – um...
Aaaaafter!

THEMBI   We did not understand a word we were saying. This 'Jack and Jill'… What did it have to do with my world? I waited to share my Gogo's [Grandmother's] rhyme. I waited – but no one asked.

(She jumps from the box, into a dynamic rendition of her grandmother's rhyme. The rhythm and vibrancy is markedly different to the banality of 'Jack and Jill'.)

Yebuya hobhe! / Uyob'uphetheni? / Ngiyobe ngipheth'inja.*

[Hey Dove! / What have you got? / I have some meat!]

Uyob'uyosaphi? / Ngiyobe ngiyoyosa endle! / Ekhaya Kunani?

[Where are you going to cook it? / Out in the field! / Why not at home?]

Ngesab'obaba! / Bazo ngephuca, basul'izindevu zomtomdala.

[I'm scared the old men will take it! / Old people, with long beards.]

Ehlez' efusini. / Eqhobonyeka! / Ethi maye! Maye! / Kazi ngoshonaphi?

[Sitting on the grass. / Boastful! / Tell me, hey! Go! / Where will I go?]

Ngoshona kobaba, eMgungundlovu. / Bangiph'ucwephe / lwakwaMasasasa

[To my father, in Mgungundlovu. / He will give you a little bit / From Masasasa]

Masasasa vuka! / Ngivuke njani? / Ngibulewe nje! / Abafana nje,

[Masasasa wake up! / How can I wake up? / I have been beaten! / By the boys,]

BakwaThabede! / Thabede muphi? / Yena losenhla!

[From Thabede! / Which Thabede? / The one from the north!]

Shay'inkomo le – Idundubale kwezikaNkeshe! / uNkesh'athini?

[Lead the cow – to the Nkeshe's! / And what will Nkeshe say?]

Angakushayi ngenduku yakhe! / Emazomb'uzombana!

[He will beat you up with the stick! / A very crooked stick!]

This was not the last time I would wait for something I already had…

* Words from a nursery rhyme taught to Thembi by her grandmother in Sabhoza Village. Original source is unknown

It was not the last time I would have to learn that there is nothing as rich as where you come from.

(*She hums the Ncede tune to herself, looking at the sky for the appearance of the bird.*)

CHILD THEMBI (*Seeing Ncede in a tree.*)

Hawu [Hey] Ncede! I wanted to tell you something:

Today I saw umlungu [a white person] – a white man – for the first time… He was waiting to drive the Nyuluka Bus [New Look Bus] back to Durban. He was kneeling down next to the bus and writing something down. And he looked very important – but he didn't know his pipi [penis] was sticking out of his shorts and sleeping on his leg – like this. (*She sticks her tongue out to rest on her cheek.*)

I thought he was an albino, like Ndundundu [the name of the albino who lived in Thembi's village] here in our village – but Mkhulu [Grandfather] says, 'No! uMlungu!' [a white person!] Mkhulu says he's from another tribe here in Africa – but they call themselves *Eulopeans* [Europeans]. (*Shrugging off her confusion.*) Ah, I don't understand these grown up things. (*Back to business.*) Anyway Ncede – I have counted all the moons in my hands. Go tell Mama and Baba it's two full moons before *Chlismas*. Tell them I'm waiting for my presents! Hambe Ncede! [Go Ncede!] Fly! (*Calling after the bird.*) And tell that moon to hurry up! I don't like it when it's half!

(*Wistfully.*) Sabhoza: where there was no electricity, but the moon and stars would light our way home.

CHILD THEMBI   (*Staring up at the night sky.*) Ah! There's the Woman in the Moon. She's carrying firewood on her head and a baby on her back – with a small dog following her.

Gogo [Granny] told me she was banished to the moon a long time ago – for working on a Sunday. She's stuck there now forever... waiting to come home.

THEMBI   Sabhoza! Where the doves spoke to us in words...

(*She imitates the sounds of the birds chirping which evolve into the imagined conversations of the birds.*)

CHILD THEMBI   Amdokwe-amabele-avuthiwe.
[The-sorgum-is-ripe-and-ready.]
Sondelani-sizodlala-sizosutha.
[Come-around-to-eat-and-play.]

THEMBI   Where we sucked morning dew from mfomfo [indigenous flower] flowers until our little faces were red from the pollen! Izinkele [indigenous berry] were our best! But they used to make us so constipated.

CHILD THEMBI   (*Whimpering in pain and holding her backside.*)
Gogo, agukakeki! [Granny, I can't shit!] I can't shit!

(*GRANDMOTHER grabs the child and puts her over her knee.*)

YAEL FARBER & THEMBI MTSHALI-JONES

GRANNY   Woza lapha! Kade nginitshela ngithi ningadli
          izinkele!
          [Come here! I have been telling you children not to eat so
          many izinkele!]

THEMBI   And she would give us her home made enema – asichathe
         [enema] – until we would shit it all out – only to run straight
         back to the forest for more!

         Supoza! Where on a Sunday in our church, people would sing
         and fall into trances.

              (*She falls into a fervent trance, speaking 'in tongues',
              imitating the adults at church gatherings.*)

         And Mkhulu [Grandfather] told us it was the language spoken in
         Heaven.

         Oh Sabhoza! I remember all your blessings… But mostly – I
         remember waiting.

              (*She sings.*)

         ───────────────────────────

         Wozani Makholwa – Jabulani Nonke,*
         [Come all ye faithful – joyful and truimphant,]
         Wozani, Wozani eBetlehem.
         [O come ye, O come ye to Bethlehem.]

         ───────────────────────────

              (*As she sings, she counts the months on her ten fingers
              – arriving triumphantly at December on her second toe.
              She stares with anticipation into the distance, looking for
              Mama and Papa on the horizon.*)

         * The text to the Christmas Carol 'O Come All Ye Faithful' was originally
         written in Latin 'Adeste Fideles' and is attributed to John Wade, an
         Englishman. The music was composed by fellow Englishman John
         Reading in the early 1700s.

THEMBI   Christmas was always very special – with my parents coming to visit. I would wish those two weeks would never end… But they always did.

(*She stares down the dust road, waving to her departing parents.*)

MAMA   (*Calling back to her.*) Don't cry Thembi! We'll be back next Christmas!

(*She waves until they are out of sight. Holding back her tears, she picks up the shoe box at her feet. Inside is a pair of small white shoes. She mimes slipping her feet into them – but finds that they are too tight for her.*)

CHILD THEMBI   (*Hobbling.*) These *Chlismas* [Christmas] shoes are small again! And Mama and Baba have gone back to Durban. Why can't people live together? Why must they go far away?

(*She comforts herself, singing a traditional Zulu lullaby in the absence of her mother.*)

Thula mntwana – Umam'akekho*

[Don't cry little one – Mama is not around]

Uyothez' amalongwe – Bath'udl'amasi

[She is getting firewood – They say you ate amasi

(sour milk mixed with cornmeal)]

Engadliwe uwe – Edliwe inja

[But you did not – The dog ate it]

Inja ka gogo – Emabalabala

[Granny's dog – with mixed colours]

---

* A traditional indigenous Zulu lullaby

THEMBI Whenever we went down to the river to fetch water, we would gather some clay to make our dolls. Babies made of earth with our little hands, and moulded from our spirits.

> (*She digs in the mound of river sand – pre-set stage left – and pulls out the parts of a small clay doll, which she begins to assemble.*)

CHILD THEMBI (*Pretending to breastfeed the doll.*)
Ufun'ukuncela?
[Do you want some milk?]

(*Pointing to her breasts.*)
I thought these were boils, but Gogo [Granny] says it's natural for them to grow, and that I must push them together so that they don't grow far apart.

Uchamelani! [You have wet yourself!]
Ngizokushaya! [I am going to beat you!] My sister Thandi from the city, her doll is pink with long hair and made of rubber from China. You can throw her on the ground and she never breaks.

(*To doll.*) But I have to be careful with you… Or you will break!

THEMBI These were dry and fragile babies – never with us for long. And so we learnt how to crumble our little creations each day and return them to the river from whence they came. Return them to the Earth, and walk away.

Babies to make, babies to hold, babies to break.

> (*She sings the opening theme – as she puts the small Christmas shoes back in the shoe box. She closes the lid of*

the large crate too – for it will soon become the bus upon
which she will ride to Durban.)

And so each new moon brought a new month. Each New Year brought me a little closer to going to live with my parents. And early one morning as I woke, my Gogo said to me:

GRANNY   Mtanomtanami [my Grandchild], … Mkhulu,
                your Grandfather has gone to the store to
                buy the flour for your dumplings. You must
                catch the chicken for your umphako [provisions
                for the journey]. Durban is a long way!

(She jumps up and down, clapping her hands with delight.)

CHILD THEMBI   I'm going to Durban! I'm going to live with
                my mama!
                I'm going to Durban! Ngiyahamba ngiya
                eThekwini!
                Ngiyahamba ngiya eThekwini! Ngiyahamba
                ngiya eThekwini! [I'm going to Durban! I'm
                going to Durban! I'm going to Durban!]

(She climbs onto the crate, which has become the Nyuluka Bus. She bounces and sways, suggesting the movements of the road travel.)

THEMBI   This was the longest journey I had ever known. I was sick from the movement of the Nyuluka Bus and the petrol fumes. I couldn't even eat my chicken and dumplings! Mostly I was sick with excitement! But when I saw my mama waiting at the station…

          (A giant suspended dress, accompanied by boisterous township jazz of the 1950s, swings on stage from the wings. THEMBI leaps off the bus and runs to embrace the dress.

She is dwarfed by this figure, which represents her mother.)

I knew my waiting was over, and from now – I would have Mama with me all the time!

CHILD THEMBI   (*With great joy.*) MAMA!

(*The music shifts and becomes more frenetic. She turns and stares at the urban chaos before her. This is Kwamashu Township – an astonishing sight for a 'rural' child.*)

THEMBI   Kwamashu Township shocked me: The closeness of houses, the closeness of everything. People here were wild. They walked too fast and talked too loud. I thought everyone's name here was 'Voetsek [Piss off] Motherfucker!'

> *(She enacts a collage of different characters from Kwamashu Township's community.)*

MAN   *(Chasing a taxi.)*
Hey mfana!
[Hey you boy!]
Nqanda leyo taxi wena!
[Stop that taxi for me!]

OLD LADY   *(Talking to a child.)* Ntombazane, yami gijima uyothenga uye estolo.
[My girl, run to the store for me.]
Uthenge uParafin iprimus stofe iyacima!
[Get me some paraffin before my primus stove switches off!]

GANGSTER   *(Propositioning a young woman.)* Ek se wena!
[I say – you!]
Woza la, ngikushele!
[Come here, I want you to be my girl!]

WOMAN   *(In response.)*
Habe, ucabanga ukuthi ngiqoma otsotsi mina!
[Hey you cheap gangster, I don't go out with thugs!]
Ungibheke kahle.
[You must watch who you are talking to!]
Sis! Gha! [Expressions of disgust or contempt]

(She imitates the sound and movements of a train.)

THEMBI   My mama took me on the Kuchu-Kuchu [colloquial onomatopoeic name for train] Train to the Durban City Indian Market.

(She disappears behind MAMA – the giant suspended dress – and peeps tentatively out, to stare open-mouthed at the scene before her.)

This was the ugliest beauty I had ever seen.

Indians everywhere, selling anything my little head could think of!

INDIAN TRADER   Ngena lapha! Yena shibhile lapha!
[Come in here! Everything is cheap here!]
One and six shillings
[British currency was used when South Africa was a colony]

For you Mama – a perfect fit!
You don't even need to try it on!

THEMBI   I had never seen so many people together in one place, and I could feel them *(Looking down at her feet where she feels the vibrations.)* – zzzzzzzzzzzz – buzzing like bees. Everyone seemed lost in this big city with so many streets, and asking for directions.

INDIAN MAN   OK! You want Curry Road?

You go down, down, down this road – you see a house on your left and a woman hanging clothes. You say hullo hullo, if you like. If you don't – you pass! You go up, up, up – you see the big Sunday [Church] with the cross on top… It's none-of-your-business!

You pass! Then you go down, down, down and you see a man standing. You ask where Curry Road is. He don't know... Come back to me! I'll show you!

CHILD THEMBI   Siyabonga! [Thank you!]

THEMBI   I had never seen so many cars in my life. In our village, there was only one car, and it belonged to the Chief. But here – every umlungu [white person] is a Chief.

They are *all* driving cars!

(*The chaos of hooters and aggression reaches a crescendo and then fades.*)

When I came to Durban to live with my parents – I thought the waiting was over, but it had only just begun. My father had abandoned my mother, to raise my brothers and sisters on her own. But Mama was hardly ever home – working day and night in the 'Kitchens'. [Colloquial term used by Domestic Workers to describe the white suburbs – as their work was invariably in the kitchens.] And so I found myself waiting once again...for her return in the evenings.

(*She stares anxiously down the road, and runs to* MAMA *when she sees her on the horizon.*)

CHILD THEMBI   Nang'uMama!
[There's Mama!]

(*Talking to the giant suspended dress which conjures her mother.*) Mama ungiphatheleni namhlanje? [Mama what did you bring for me today?]

YAEL FARBER & THEMBI MTSHALI-JONES

MAMA   Oh mtanaam, ngikhathele!
              [Oh child, I'm tired!]
              I'm so tired. I'm going straight to bed.

CHILD THEMBI (*Calling after her.*) OK Ma – we can talk in
              the morning.

THEMBI   But each day, when we woke, she was gone – already on her
         way back to the Kitchens. Waiting for our precious moment
         on Sunday in church – standing next to her, I would watch her
         sing her favourite hymn.

              (*Enacting her mother in church – she sings with a glorious
              voice, as the giant dress swings from side to side.*)

MAMA

              _____

              Endleleni yami*
              [Everywhere I go]
              Wongiphumelelisa
              [He protects me]
              Ofana noJesu
              [Someone like Jesus]
              Ngomtholaphi
              [Will never be found]

              _____

THEMBI   I was so proud I belonged to her. When she told me I could
         come with her to the Kitchens one day to help her with the
         washing – I could hardly wait. It meant spending more time
         with her.

              (*Humming, she enacts* MAMA, *cleaning the home of her
              white employer.*)

         * Lyrics from a spiritual / hymn 'Endleni Yami' traditionally sung in
         Church.

MAMA   Thembi, I am going to clean the bedrooms.
                 Wait for me here – and please mtanaam [my
                 child] don't touch anything.

CHILD THEMBI   Kulungile Ma. [OK Mama.]

(*She climbs onto the crate and waits.*)

THEMBI   I waited in that kitchen the whole afternoon, and felt very
         uncomfortable wherever I sat. But there are some things in this
         world that *cannot* wait!

CHILD THEMBI   Ngifun'ukuchama!
                 [I need to pee!]

THEMBI   I needed to wee!

(*She waits, but it is unbearable. She climbs off the crate and
ventures beyond the kitchen.*)

CHILD THEMBI   Ma? Mama? (*But there is no response.*)

(*A gleaming white porcelain toilet is revealed centre stage.*)

(*Delighted at her discovery.*)
Ah! iToilet!

(*With great relief she hurries to the toilet, mimes hitching
up her dress and pulling down her panties. She sits on the
toilet.*)

(*Imitating the sound of her sudden bladder
release.*) SHWAAH!

THEMBI   It felt so good to wee at last!

When suddenly…coming through the door…I saw a huge belly.

CHILD THEMBI   (*Pushing the door closed.*) Sorry! Somebody's here!

THEMBI   I said!… Because I thought I was a 'somebody'. But Mr Big Belly did not agree.

MR BOSS   (*Furious.*) Margaret! MAAARGREEEET!

THEMBI   My mama dropped whatever she was doing and came running.

MAMA   (*Out of breath, frightened.*) What is it, Baas? [Boss]

What happened, Master? [The term Master was and is still commonly used by black employees when addressing their white employers.]

MR BOSS   (*Outraged.*) WHO is in my toilet?

MAMA   (*Submissively.*) Oh, it's my daughter Baas.

MR BOSS   Your WHO?

MAMA   My daughter, Baas.

MR BOSS   (*Yelling with rage.*) YOUR WHO? You girls – you KNOW you're not supposed to use MY toilet! You must use the toilet OUTSIDE! [It was and remains common for black women of mature age to be called 'girls' by those expressing racial superiority]

MAMA   (*Rhythmically, cowering with submission.*)
                Yes Baas. No Baas. She just didn't know Baas!
                Yes Baas. No Baas. I'll explain it to her now!

THEMBI   I had never heard anyone speak to my mother like that before.
          I had never heard my mama apologising like that.

MAMA   Yes Baas. No Baas. She just didn't know Baas!
                Yes Baas. No Baas. I'll explain it to her now!

                (*During the above, the large suspended dress starts to droop
                and slowly crumples to the ground. CHILD THEMBI runs to
                the dress – now a limp pile on the floor.*)

CHILD THEMBI   uXolo, Ma! uXolo! [I'm sorry, Mama! I'm sorry!]
                I didn't know!

THEMBI   This toilet was of such great importance. I didn't know. It had
          swallowed up my mother. Where did she go? (*Peering into the
          toilet.*) Where had my mama gone?

          The woman who stood so strong! And who…

                (*She pulls a tiny version of the dress from the toilet bowl.*)

          …was this small woman…singing this strange song:

                (*On her knees – she holds the small dress in front of her. The
                effect dwarfs her.*)

MAMA   Yes Baas. No Baas. She just didn't know Baas!
                Yes Baas. No Baas. I'll explain it to her now!

THEMBI   (*Rising to her feet to address the audience.*) For all of us, the day
          comes when we must look our mother in the eye, and realise
          that she is human after all. But that day, I looked my mama in

the eye too soon. Not because I had grown tall… But because, in that house – she had been made small.

(*She sings slowly and softly.*)

Endleleni yami
[Every where I go]
Wongiphumelelisa
[He protects me]
Ofana noJesu
[Someone like Jesus]
Ngomtholaphi
[Will never be found]

(*She walks to the crumpled dress, kneels beside it and tenderly spreads it out before her.*)

All the excitement I came to Durban with died in me that summer. I began to understand the reality of what my mama had to go through to buy me that little pair of shoes that never fitted… The reality of what life held for me. As my high school years passed – I became shy and silent. My spirit was still searching for a place to settle in this city. I had no friends except for a young man who showed some interest in me. And before I knew it, they told me I was carrying a child!

I did not even know where it came from. No one had explained these things to me. No one had time. She was too busy trying to feed seven hungry mouths.

(*She sings.*)

Endleleni yami
[Everywhere I go]
Wongiphumelelisa
[He protects me]
Ofana noJesu

[Someone like Jesus]

Ngomtholaphi

[Will never be found]

———————————

(She sings softly as she moves away from the dress to centre stage.)

Durban! Thekwini! Manz'eTeko! [Vernacular names for the city of Durban]

Where on a hot summer night, you could taste the salt and blood on the air;
Where white beaches are marked with black oil stains that no one could clean;
Houses with toilets of such big importance…that they could swallow a woman…

City of Bees… You stung me.

(*THEMBI wears a standard pink Domestic Worker's uniform – with apron and frilly white trimming – the signature look of millions of women who earn their living in South Africa, by minding children more privileged than their own. She holds a velvet brown bundle which symbolises her newborn daughter, PHUMZILE.*)

THEMBI   The first time I held my child in my arms – I knew I was touching the most dangerous moment of my life. I knew it was dangerous to love anything so much. But Phumzi… (*Addressing her daughter, PHUMZILE, in her mind.*) Nothing… nothing prepared me for the pain of leaving you at home, to go and look after someone else's child.

> (*She sings the closing phrase of a lullaby to her child, and lays her down.*)

Inja ka gogo

[Granny's dog]

Emabalabala

[With mixed colours]

> (*A phrase of traditional Zulu guitar chords shifts the tempo of the scene, as the lights suggest the early morning rising sun. She is standing at a bus stop with other domestic workers, waiting for the morning bus.*)

20 YR THEMBI   Where is this Putco Bus? Late again as usual!

OLD WORKER   These skorokoro [scraps] buses are always breaking down!

YOUNG WORKER   Nkosiyami! [My God!] My madam!

I'm going to find her waiting for me at the front door.

20 YR THEMBI   Ah! Here it comes!

(*She sits on the up-turned zinc bath, suggesting she has boarded the bus. She holds tightly to her 'seat' for the chaotic drive ahead.*)

THEMBI   Seven am Point Road Putco to the Durban Beachfront: baby blue in colour, and farting diesel all the way down Marine Parade… Carrying aprons and doeks [head scarves] on their way to the Kitchens to earn their daily bread. It was a shaking bus, a shouting bus… A-Mother's-Love-for-Hire Bus.

(*She recedes deep into thought, and addresses her newborn child.*)

Phumzile, I hated leaving you each Monday morning – especially when you cried… I would carry the sound of your voice with me for the whole week.

OLD WORKER   (*To THEMBI, interrupting her thoughts.*)
Hey Ntombazane! [Girl!] Better put a smile on that face. Madam doesn't want a sulky girl.

(*She arrives at the home of the family she is working for. The mother of the child she is employed to care for – her 'madam' – is tapping her foot impatiently.*)

MADAM   What's your story today, my 'girl'? Why are you late? You can't keep me waiting like this! There are lots of 'girls' looking for jobs, you know! Samantha's had her morning feed. I'll be back by five.

(*MADAM hands a six-month old baby to THEMBI.*

All the children in this scene are represented by child figures,
constructed from empty clothing that retains the form of a
child, but the figure is hollow – thus functioning symbolically
rather than literally.)

20 YR THEMBI   Thank you Madam. I'm sorry Madam.

It won't happen again.

(*She sighs with relief once* MADAM *is gone. Her rapport*
with the baby is warm and genuinely loving.)

Hullo Sammy! Hello 'Nana'! [Affectionate
non-sensical term for a small child] Oh look you're
smiling today! (*Mischievously.*) Not like your
mummy!

(*She begins to sing a traditional lullaby, and secures the*
child to her back in the traditional manner, with a blanket
wrapped at her waist. She gathers the dirty laundry in a
large zinc tub and begins the washing.)

Shoo! [Wow!] iWashing engaka! [So much
washing!]

Kanti labelungu babhuquzaphi odakeni?
[Are these white people rolling themselves in mud?]

THEMBI   (*Addressing her daughter in her mind's eye once again.*)

Phumzile,

We began our journey together, the day you made a movement
in my stomach. I had no idea babies could move under their
mother's skin. At that time, you were my secret alone…my
little kicking secret. I would lie awake at night worrying that
my sleeping position was uncomfortable for you. I remember
counting the passing of full moons – nine of them – before

we met. I had planned to look beautiful for our first moment together – but you didn't give me a chance to braid my hair before going to the hospital.

Like all things unborn – the ghost of waiting had not yet come to you.

> (*She wrings out the washing in the tub. The breathing and motion suggest the effort of giving birth.*)

(*Holding a garment of child's clothing, looking at it tenderly.*) So fragile – brownish little face with a mouth like a little bird… I wanted to sing for you the Dove Song that my grandmother taught me as a girl.

> (*She sings to the newborn child she recalls in her hands.*)

Khele, Khele Nkoviyo! / Uphetheni ngomlomo?
[Hey there big owl! / What are you carrying with your mouth?]

Ngipheth'amas'omtwana. / Uwasaphi na?
[I'm carrying my baby's food. / Where are you taking it?]

Ngiwasa kozong'nceda. / Ancendeni na?
[To someone who will help me. / Help you with what?]

> (*She rises from her kneeling position, with the child asleep on her back. She goes 'outside' to hang the washing to dry. The phone rings, and she hurries back inside.*)

20 YR THEMBI   (*Answering the phone.*) Hullo?

(*Submissively.*) Oh! Madam! I was outside hanging the washing… (*Listening.*) Yes Madam… (*Listening.*) I know you don't want anyone calling me here… (*Listening.*) No Madam! I won't open the door for anybody… (*Listening.*) Oh no madam! I won't carry the baby on my back…

THEMBI   By lunchtime, my breasts would be full of milk and aching.

(*The child on her back begins to cry.*)

20 YR THEMBI   Ssh! You hungry Sammy? OK 'Moenchie Moenchie'. [Affectionate non-sensical term for a child]

I'm going to feed you just now.

(*She takes the child off her back and begins to unbutton her uniform.*)

OK, Sammy! Don't cry baby.

Your milk is coming now.

(*She lays the child down, and moves to the toilet out in the yard. She leans over and squeezes her breast milk into the toilet bowl, wincing with pain. The child's cries become increasingly distressed.*)

Please baby, just hang on.

I won't be long. Your milk is coming now.

Don't cry Sweetie. I'm coming soon.

(*When she has relieved the milk from her breasts, she hurries back to Samantha, giving her a bottle of formula milk.*)

I'm sorry Sammy. Here's your milk, nana.

Oh, you were hungry. I'm so sorry you had to wait!

(*The child gulps the milk down. THEMBI sings softly to her, and then drifts to thoughts of PHUMZILE.*)

THEMBI   (*Radiant with the memory.*)
The first time you sucked my titties for your milk, was a
surprise to me that you already knew what to do. Who told
you? How did you know? My breasts were burning with pain,
but I was enjoying the fact that you knew you were supposed
to suck out your milk. I wanted to boast to the whole world
how clever my child was. Phumzi – you were always waiting
for your mama's milk.

> (*Getting up and directly addressing the audience, holding
> the figure of the white child.*)

This child was a job like any other. But when you spend
every hour of the day together, it's impossible not to become
attached to one another. Somewhere beyond the madams, the
dirty washing, the backrooms, and bad wages…

Was a child that depended on you for everything! Just a
child…

I have held many babies in my time. Who knows? I might
have held one of you.

> (*She takes a second child's figure from the smaller wooden
> crate she has been sitting on.*)

Some I cared for with my hands…

> (*She takes out a third child.*)

And some I cared for with my heart. But at any moment, you
could be told you were no longer needed. And so I would have
to take my love, pack it away, and unpack it for the next child
I cared for.

> (*She takes a small boy figure by the hand.*)

20 YR THEMBI   Come Shaun. Don't you want to go to the park?

(*She leans down to listen to what the child says to her.*)

Of course I'll stay with you. I'm not going to leave you. I'll be with you all the time.

Now, don't run too fast.

(*The child falls. She picks him up and holds him with great tenderness.*)

Sorry Baby! Don't cry.

(*She places the boy – as if on a swing – and rocks him.*)

Sit here and hold on tight.

THEMBI   (*Addressing PHUMZILE in her mind, as she swings the small boy.*)

Wo-Hey Phumzi! I would wonder the whole week what you were doing at home. Were you finishing your food? Were you taking your bottle? Or was my sister Thandi still giving you her empty breast for comfort? I envied the little white children I cared for. They had everything…including me! Whenever I played games with them, I would wish you were here too. But you were playing on the dusty streets of Kwamashu.

(*To the audience.*) By the end of the week – the waiting was the worst. Waiting for the family to finish dinner, so I could clear the table…

20 YR THEMBI   (*Collecting a dish.*) Thank you Master.

THEMBI Wash up and finally go home to my child.

Waiting for the child to fall asleep in the evenings when her parents were out…

20 YR THEMBI   (*Holding the child, rocking her to sleep.*) Ssssh. I'm just going to the kitchen. I'll leave the door open.

OK, sssh! Don't worry. I'll stay here with you.

(*The phone rings.*)

Yes Madam… She's falling asleep…

(*Distressed.*) You're going to be late? What time?

But it's Friday. I'm supposed to go home tonight.

I'll miss my nine o'clock bus… I…but…

(*Resigned.*) OK, madam – I'll wait.

(*She puts down the phone and whispers to the child who has woken and is now crying for its mother.*)

Its OK, baby… Don't cry. Mummy's coming home soon.

THEMBI   (*To PHUMZILE in her mind.*) I'm coming home soon Phumzi.

Please wait for me if you can. I'm coming soon.

(*She begins to sing the child her old Zulu lullaby.*)

———————————

Thula mntwana! Umam'akekho.

[Don't cry little one! Mama is not around.]

YAEL FARBER & THEMBI MTSHALI-JONES

Uyothez' amalongwe. Bath'udl'amasi

[She is getting firewood. They say you ate 'amasi'.]

Engadliwe uwe! Edliwe inja!

[But you did not! The dog ate it!]

Inja ka gogo – Emabalabala.

[Granny's dog – with mixed colours.]

(*She lays the child down and stands to leave. As she crosses the stage – she peels away the house coat and apron she has worn. Arriving 'home' at the large wooden crate, she picks up the small velvet bundle that is* PHUMZILE. *She caresses and holds her with great emotion. They lie down together to sleep.*)

20 YR THEMBI   (*Looking at the full moon outside the window, whispers.*)

Look there Phumzi! It's the woman in the moon!

She's stuck there, waiting to come home.

But soon Phumzi…soon…

(*She falls asleep, holding her child.*)

(*Suddenly, there is a violent knock at the door. It is the* BLACK JACK *Municipal Workers – assigned to search people's houses in the township – hoping to catch those staying 'illegally' in areas they do not have a permit for.*)

BLACK JACK   Vula! VULA! [Open! OPEN!]

OPEN UP! VULA UMNYANGO! [OPEN THE DOOR!]

THEMBI   Night raids were a common thing in the townships – as the Black Jack Municipal Workers would barge into houses checking for House Permits in the middle of the night.

(*The BLACK JACK moves around the large wooden crate, shining his torch though through the windows and knocking on the walls.*)

BLACK JACK   VULA VULA! [OPEN! OPEN!]

OPEN UP OR WE'LL BREAK THIS DOOR DOWN!!!

(*The lid of the box opens onto the ground as though the front door has been wrenched open. THEMBI stands in the doorway holding PHUMZILE. The following is a rapid series of questions and demands from the BLACK JACK – delivered aggressively, as the actress switches between the role of THEMBI and the interrogator.*)

Why didn't you open the door? Who are you hiding?

Whose are all these children?

Where's the house permit?

NTOMBAZANA! [GIRL!]

WHERE IS THE HOUSE PERMIT?

20 YR THEMBI   (*Terrified.*) I don't know where my mother keeps it.

BLACK JACK   PHUMA! [GO!] OUTSIDE! You are coming with us.

20 YR THEMBI   What about my baby? I can't leave her.

BLACK JACK   You are coming – with or without the baby!

Handing PHUMZILE to a member of the audience.

YAEL FARBER & THEMBI MTSHALI-JONES

20 YR THEMBI	Thandi (*Thembi's sister*) take Phumzile!
	If I don't come back… (*But she is interrupted.*)
BLACK JACK	NTOMBAZANA! [GIRL!] LET'S GO!

(*She is brutally shoved into the truck. The large crate now serves as the police van, with* THEMBI *clambering onto the top, to create the impression of being in the back of the vehicle.*)

THEMBI   (*To the audience.*) Everyone is quiet here. Everyone is thinking about their own problems: the children who will not have breakfast before school; the jobs that everyone will be late for. We drive from house to house, from section to section. The truck is getting fuller and fuller. It's beginning to stink in here. It smells of alcohol and farts, of sleep and fear. Two o'clock comes and goes…three am – four – five… All I can think of is my baby. She has missed her night feed.

(*To* PHUMZILE *in despair.*) Phumzile, what am I doing in the back of this truck in the middle of the night. I am supposed to be in bed with you. These are our only precious moments together.

(*To audience.*) We arrive at Kwamashu Township Office. They open the van.

BLACK JACK	Phumani! [Out!] Out! Out!

THEMBI   (*Blinded by the morning sun after the night in the dark van.*) The sun is already up.

BLACK JACK	Woza Ntombazana! [Come girl!] Next!
	Your name! Your address! Your birth date!

20 YR THEMBI	Thembekile Heavygale Mtshali. F89.
	November 7th 1949.
BLACK JACK	(*After checking his register.*) Hamba! [Go!] Next!

THEMBI I am released. I have not washed, I have not fed my baby and…

20 YR THEMBI	(*Looking at her watch.*)
	Oh Nkosi yami! [My God!] I am two hours late for work!
MADAM	(*Smoking and highly annoyed.*)
	So what is it this time, my girl? Oh let me guess! Putco Bus was late again! No, no… one of your brothers died. Who killed who this time? What? My girl – I have heard stories from you, but this one takes the cake! Next time you want to sleep late with your boyfriends try and think of something a bit more believable!

(*MADAM drops her cigarette and crushes it with her foot.*)

THEMBI (*Turning to the audience.*) 'Believable!' I could not have come up with this story if I had tried: dragging sleeping men, women and children out of their beds in the middle of the night – to check if a piece of paper says they have the right to be in their own homes?

20 YR THEMBI	Yes madam. I'm sorry madam. It won't happen again! I'll wash the clothes and iron them!

YAEL FARBER & THEMBI MTSHALI-JONES

Wash the carpets too. Wash the b
the curtains… Wash myself…of

(*She begins to do the washing in the zin
sings. Her movements extend from washing the clothes to
scrubbing her own arms, neck and face. The song builds in
intensity until it is an emotional and moving lament. She
stands, moves to the washing line, and pegs her Domestic
Worker's Uniform onto the line. She steps into the dress, and
appears suspended from the washing line. She steps away
from the line, now wearing the uniform.*)

THEMBI (*To PHUMZILE.*)

Phumzile:

There is time lost that I mourn. Time I can never reclaim. I
would give up a list of things I have treasured most: loves,
friends, productions, my worldly goods. I would give all this
and more – if I could only travel backwards in time to your
first years… To rewrite the hours that I encouraged words
from the mouth of someone else's child – while you said
your first 'mama' and I was not there to celebrate it. If I had
the power – I would trade the moments I walked someone
else's child in the park, while you took your first steps on this
earth – and I was not there to throw you up in the air and call
you a queen. But it is gone this time, and I can never trade it
back. Not for anything I have to offer. And I must make peace
with this heart…

And these hand…that held another child…

While you – Phumzi…

Waited for me.

With Love, Mama

(She peels the uniform from her and drops it to the floor, and sings.)

———————————

My sister breast-fed my baby*
While I took care of you
We met when you were three months old
And I a woman of twenty-two.
Your mother put you in my arms
And I wrapped you to my back
Your pink cheek on my neck
Was tender as a lover's.
I was your only resting place
You seemed to want no other
Your first word was my name
Your first song was in Zulu.
I was standing right beside you
When you stood and took your first step
I slept on the floor beside your bed
Three times a week
And when you woke from a dangerous dream
I sang you back to sleep.
On Sunday when I went home
You followed me to the gate
Your father bought an ice-cream cone
To help you to forget
On Monday morning I was back
To greet you when you woke
And when you woke
My children breathed tear gas smoke
While I took care of you.
Your eyes are bright and clever now
Your legs are straight and strong
You're a boy who runs and jumps and climbs

* Song lyrics to 'My Sister Breastfed my Baby' written by Barney Simon with Thembi Mtshali-Jones

You go to school on your own
Your hair is like your mother's
You have your father's face
Sometimes I wonder what you'll be
When you're a man.
A cowboy like you've always dreamt
A spaceman, a doctor, a lawyer
The choice is yours mntanami [my child]
But I pray I never see you
In the uniform of a soldier
Riding through Soweto streets
High above in a casspir
My children make petrol bombs
While I take care of you
My children sing at funerals
While I take care of you
Mntanami – child of my flesh
May God protect my children from you

FOUR • THIS MUSEUM IN ME

(The stage is clear, but for the gleaming white porcelain toilet – upon which she is seated centre stage.)

THEMBI *(Addressing, in her mind's eye, the man who banished her from his toilet in her childhood.)*

Dear Mr Boss,

You may not remember me…but I am *(Looking up at the audience with a smile.)* ME!

The little girl you kicked out of your toilet. And since she last saw you – she has seen many other toilets in her life – from the toilets of the township, to the cream and brass fittings of international hotels. And from all the toilets I've seen in my life, I've learnt one thing alone: that a toilet is just a toilet…no matter who is sitting on it. I never saw your face. Just your big belly, as it pushed through the door and into my world forever. A world that expected me to inherit a legacy of dirty dishes and other people's children. This little girl, whose bum was too black for your white toilet seat – made it out of the kitchens and onto the stage…

Because God, Mr Boss, works in mysterious ways. The last family I worked for – had a daughter Charlene. She saw beyond the girl in the kitchen. She saw me! And with her faith, she changed my destiny.

She would listen to me singing as I was cooking, washing and cleaning the house.

She came to me with a newspaper advert and encouraged me to audition for a theatre production. She was more excited than me when I got the part, and offered to wash the dishes for me so that I could perform each night.

76 YAEL FARBER & THEMBI MTSHALI-JONES

(She sings the opening lines of the lead song of the musical Ipi Ntombi, *made famous internationally during the 1970s. She closes the toilet seat with a flourish and pushes it off stage and out of her life.)*

Tonight, tonight's a wedding feast*
The men arrive with a slaughtered beast
A wail, a chant soon fills the air
For miles around they'll hear the sound.

It's no mystery I waited until now to get married. For a while I thought I'd used up all my wedding vows in *Ipi Ntombi* and my ancestors eventually went on strike… After being called to bless my wedding for four years – every night!

(She sings.)

Mama Thembu's getting married tonight†
All the spirits will be chanting their delight
Mama Thembu's getting married tonight
The bones are thrown and mama's path is very bright…

Of all the productions I've done, *Ipi Ntombi* lived with me the longest. It was the production that brought me to Johannesburg, and I had to bring Phumzile with me.

(She fetches a small pair of school shoes and small brown school suitcase.)

1976 was the year Phumzile started school.

---

* Lyrics extracted from the South African musical *Ipi Ntombi* by Gail Lakier & Bertha Egnos 1975

† Ibid

25 YR THEMBI   (*To PHUMZILE, as the child leaves for her first day of school.*)

Hamba kahle mntanami!

[Go well my child.]

Uqaphele izimoto!

[Be careful of the cars!]

I'll be waiting for you when you come home.

(*She places the shoes and school bag centre stage.*)

It was also the year the children of Soweto stopped waiting…

(*She sings.*)

———————————

As night fades out…
Faded by the sun
Ten thousand kids stood high on the hill…

———————————

THEMBI   But the show went on!

(*She dances around the small school shoes and suitcase, singing.*)

———————————

Oh! Lagqira lagqira laqabela phaya!*

[The traditional healer roars and jumps high!]

Oh! Lagqira lagqira laqabela phaya!

[The traditional healer roars and jumps high!]

———————————

The whites-only audience would smile and applaud, and eat their Quality Streets, before going back to their quality streets. It was a different world we would return to. Ten kilometres away – Soweto was another country… And it was burning.

* Lyrics extracted from the South African musical *Ipi Ntombi* by Gail Lakier & Bertha Egnos 1975

       YAEL FARBER & THEMBI MTSHALI-JONES

(*She kneels and lights a candle.*) We saw in every house, mothe
sitting in dim candlelight… Waiting for the sound of the door,
as their children came home.

> (*She prays for the return of the children.*)

But those doors will remain shut forever.

> (*She gathers the dust that her childhood clay doll lies in, and
> walks backwards, letting the sand pour through her fingers
> as she goes.*)

And so they crumbled their little creations, returning them to
the earth from whence they came.

And walked away…
Returned them to the earth and walked away.
Babies to make…
Babies to hold…
Babies to break.

> (*She sings softly.*)

Ipi Ntombi yami? Ntombi yami?*
[Where's my girl? My girl?]
Ipi Ntombi yami? Ntombi yami?
[Where's my girl? My girl?]

By the late seventies I had performed on the West End and
Broadway – but what is smiling and kicking your legs high on
Broadway, when your home is on fire? I knew it was time to
walk the road that other artists had paved… To use the stage to
tell the truth…

* Lyrics extracted from the South African musical *Ipi Ntombi* by Gail
Lakier & Bertha Egnos 1975

(Sings the opening lines of the song sung in the previous scene.)

My sister breastfed my baby, while I took care of you…*

One night, at The Market Theatre in Johannesburg – more than fifteen years ago, I was on stage singing. I noticed a young man in the audience in uniform, and although he was trying to hide, I could see his tears in the dark.

(Sings the closing line.)

May God protect my children from you.†

He came to my dressing room after the show.

WHITE SOLDIER   I am just finishing my army service in the townships…

THEMBI   It was during the State of Emergency in the late 80s. I thought of those fresh young faces we knew so well on the Casspirs [Military war vehicle used in the townships during the 1980s]. Those eyes that had no mercy in them. But this young man's eyes had tears in them. I had no words. I held him while he cried.

(To the memory of the soldier.) I want you to know – wherever you are – that you showed me something too that night: the damage that had been done to all of us.

(She hums gently to herself.)

And then suddenly, after all those years… It seemed the waiting was over.

---

* Lyrics extracted from 'My Sister Breastfed my Baby' written by Barney Simon with Thembi Mtshali-Jones

† Ibid

(She ululates.)

There were miracles happening off-stage:

Madiba [Xhosa clan name, which many use as a sign of respect, when referring to Nelson Mandela] walked out of jail after 27 years of waiting; I welcomed friends – like Miriam Makeba – home after 31 years in forced exile. I stood for hours in line, with my granddaughter Khanyisile – waiting to cast my vote for the first time in my life. I joined hands with the other artists at the Union Buildings in Pretoria – for the inauguration of our first democratic president – Nelson Rolihlahla Mandela!

(She sings the closing phrases of 'Nkosi sikilel' iAfrika' – a song of the struggle, and South Africa's new national anthem since democracy was won.)

SICHABA SA YESU!*
[THIS OUR LAND]
SICHABA SA SOUTH AFRICA
[THIS LAND OF SOUTH AFRICA]

But when the storm died down, and the celebrations were over… I knew the waiting was not. The silence remained. One Sunday night – as I turned my television on to watch the first of the Truth and Reconciliation Hearings…I saw it! I saw it in the eyes of the women: mothers of missing children, wives of missing men… A haunting silence of stories waiting to be told.

(She kneels and speaks to the women she saw at the testimonies.)

---

* Lyrics extracted from the hymn 'Nkosi Sikelel' iAfrika' written by Reverend Enoch Sontonga, which became a song of the struggle for freedom in South Africa, and is now South Africa's national anthem

Bomama, you sat with your backs straight – your handbags on your laps and your handkerchiefs in your sleeves. You waited with a dignity and patience that shamed all those who have never had to wait for anything.

You said nothing, but when you began to speak – you broke a lifetime of silence…

(*The below speech begins with restraint and builds steadily before resolving.*)

MOTHER   (*Testifying.*) Cha cha! Ngeke.
               [No, no! I cannot!]
               Ngizokhuluma, ngizokhuluma! Cha cha
               ngeke!
               [I will speak, I will speak! No, no I cannot!]
               No! No! My heart will burst if I speak.
               Cha cha!
               [No no! I cannot!]
               No! No! My heart will burst if I speak. Yet
               I must speak so that my heart may burst. I
               WILL speak so that my heart may burst.
               Ngizokhuluma! Ngizokhuluma!
               [I will speak! And I will speak!]
               Grief fills the room up with my absent child.
               Ubuhlungu bungidla amathumbu.
               [The pain is eating me inside.]
               Buyangidabula ngeke buze buphele uma
               ngingakhulumi!
               [It is tearing me apart and it won't stop if I need to speak!]
               I have waited for too long. He was dying my
               child, and they wouldn't let me hold him.
               Abavumanga ukuthi ngimgone.
               [They refused to let me hold him.]

This inside me fights my tongue…it fights
my tongue…my tongue…my tongue tongue
tongue my TONGUE!

(*Crying out in rage.*)

'O, that my tongue were in the thunder's
mouth!*
Then with a passion would I shake the world;
And rouse from sleep that fell anatomy
Which cannot hear a lady's feeble voice…'
Lala kahle Mtanami.
[Rest in peace my child.]
I have translated you from the dead.

(*Gently – she sings the opening theme. In a calabash she
lights 'Mphepo', a dried herb used when communing with
one's ancestors.*)

THEMBI (*Clapping her hands softly, she praises her ancestors.*)
Nina boMtshali ka Hlabangane!
[You of the Mtshali clan – son of Hlabangane!]
Bo MaGalela agase njengengonyama
[Son of Magalela: The one who fights like a lion]
Siyabonga konke enisenzele khona
[Thank you for everything you did for us.]
Nasibheka, nasibonisa indlela.
[You looked after us and paved the way.]
Siyabonga, siyabonga.
[We give thanks, we give thanks.]
We give thanks… We give thanks.

(*She looks up to face the audience.*)

* William Shakespeare's *King John*: III:i:40–44

When I walk through this museum in me, I finally understand the power of facing the past.

(*She walks to the childhood Christmas shoes and picks them up.*)

It's over half a century since that heavy gale first blew me into this world.

This little girl…

(*She holds the small shoes to her heart.*)

Who was too shy to even raise her hand in class – would find herself here tonight… Akhulume! [Speaking!] Telling my story!

(*She places the shoes before her on the floor.*)

And we *must* speak…or it will eat us inside.
We must speak…
Or our hearts will burst.

(*She raises her arms, puts her head back and sings with power and joy.*)

Thokolathemba we babe amathunz'ayewukela.*
[We must not lose hope.]
Seliya ngomtsha wendoda. Woza mama, Woza!
[It is close by. Come mama, come!]
Bath'intandane enhle ngumakhothwa unina
[You are not an orphan when you have a loving mother.]
Bayeza kusasa. Bayeza!
[The healers are coming tomorrow. They are coming!]

* Lyrics from a traditional indigenous song vocally rearranged by Thembi Mtshali-Jones

YAEL FARBER & THEMBI MTSHALI-JONES

Bayeza kusasa, bayeza!

[The healers are coming, to heal our land!]

Blackout.

AMAJUBA
LIKE DOVES WE RISE

Conceived & written by Yael Farber

I n 2000, Yael Farber arrived in Mafikeng – a tiny town in the dustbowl of South Africa's former Homeland of Bophuthatswana, where she had been commissioned by the North West Arts Council (an organisation which later merged with and became known as Mmabana Arts Foundation) to create a new theatre work. Farber planned to embark on a process of creating a piece culled from the lives of her cast, lived in the shadow of Apartheid's dying years. She was assigned the Arts Council's five resident actors, but knew nothing of the actors' biographical details prior to the first day of the creative process. Testament to the all-pervasive nature of Apartheid, Farber needed to conduct no further selective casting process based on the content of the actor's life experiences. Being black South Africans, these five artists inevitably had stories of exceptional endurance to tell. Agreeing to share personal details towards creating a biographical tapestry of life lived under Apartheid's full force, the actors embarked on an intensive process of remembrance, with Farber. Weeks in an 'aircon-less' studio at the Arts Council during that sweltering summer, saw director and actors immerse themselves in the demanding creative process. Days of intensive memory recall by the actors were captured by Farber in writing. Evenings of staging and rehearsing would follow, after which Farber would go home and script through the night, while the actors memorised moves and lines for the following day's work. A defining moment for *Amajuba* came when one of the cast members, overcome with emotion whilst recalling a memory – was given sudden reprieve from his narrative by the other cast members, who began to spontaneously sing. This is common practice at Township funerals, with song being perhaps the spiritual balm by which millions have survived unspeakable events in South Africa's past. Farber immediately determined that the narratives would be strung together on the powerful yet fragile thread of such community spirituals and songs.

After a six week period of research, creation, writing and staging – *Amajuba* was set to premiere in Mafikeng. Hours after the show was to commence, the audience slowly accumulated – perhaps due to both the calm lack of

.phasis placed on time in Mmabatho, as well as the fact that a large black snake had been sighted entering the theatre. After an intensive search which yielded nothing, the company decided to 'curtain up' – and *Amajuba: Like Doves We Rise* was born. For two years, the production played at modest festivals around South Africa, and at The State Theatre in Pretoria, South Africa. It was at the 2002 National Festival of the Arts in South Africa that Tish Francis, director of the Oxford Playhouse (who was in the process of bringing Farber's adaptation of *Julius Caesar* – *SeZaR* – to the UK) saw *Amajuba* for the first time, and was immediately passionate about presenting the work on a larger scale in the UK. In 2003, Ms Francis presented *Amajuba* for a short but highly successful season at her theatre in Oxford. An extensive tour of the UK – by The Oxford Playhouse in association with The Farber Foundry – followed in 2004. The continued investment and faith in the production by Ms Francis and The Oxford Playhouse would prove instrumental to the international profile the production would come to develop as it toured in association with The Playhouse. *Amajuba* enjoyed enormous critical and audience success as it played across the UK – from small towns, to The Barbican Theatre and The Edinburgh Festival in 2004 – winning The Angel Herald Award and transferring to the West End. The production experienced two cast member replacements during these years, which (due to its biographical nature) changed the text substantially each time. The integrity of *Amajuba* is based on the premise that Farber would re-work the text to accommodate the new testimony of any new cast member, but the core concept and remaining testimonies were untouched.

The production has gone on to play extensively and to stunning response around the world in cities across Ireland, Australia and the USA – including a critically acclaimed Off-Broadway New York City run at The Culture Project (for which a Drama Desk award nomination followed in 2007). The production continued to travel internationally under the management of *The Farber Foundry* for several years, until it was retired in 2007 – despite continued invitations from around the world to this day.

'You need only claim the events of your life to make yourself yours.'

South Africa is an extraordinary country in so many ways. Indeed the relatively peaceful transition from almost half a century of brutal oppression to democracy was nothing short of miraculous. Yet beneath the hype and sense of possibility emanating from our country lies the dark current of consequence. There are statistics and numbers that will some day speak to our grandchildren of the damage wrought by Apartheid… But the emotional devastation of those years cannot be audited. Forced Removals – while indeed socio-politically significant – on a more delicate level tore families apart, frightened children, and ruptured the fragile process of growing up. The State of Emergency declared in the 1980s – while explosive to the masses – was a shadow that fell upon countless adolescents. Instead of grappling with heady days of teenage insecurity and awakening sexuality, they were facing down war vehicles with nothing but stones and courage at 15 years old. The cold technicality of The Land Act & Group Areas Act indeed perverted the socio-economic structure of a country but the childhood years infected with poverty and relentless hunger haunt those who carry these memories today. The chillingly exact legislation of the Apartheid regime left in its wake countless lives irrevocably changed. The flexibility with which the survivors of these years have had to rise to embrace the 'new' South Africa has inspired the world – but left little time for looking back to reclaim the emotional shrapnel left from those dark years… Somewhere out there is a metaphorical scrapyard where these lost details lie – waiting to be reclaimed. It is to this shattered landscape of memory that the actors agreed to return when we embarked on the creative process of *Amajuba*. Everything they will share with you tonight is true…the intimate details of their own childhoods lived within the Apartheid divisions. Embarking on this journey, we held fast to the notion that until you go back and claim each broken piece of your past you can never be truly free. *Amajuba* is the telling of five 'small' stories plucked from the millions untold – for indeed we are a nation of too many sorrows to recount. We hope that the light of these five stories remembered will shine for the countless that will remain untold. *Amajuba* was created as a proud acknowledgement of the inexplicable hope that has continued to burn in South Africa's people – even in the darkest years. It bears testimony to the extraordinary spirituality present in our country despite the devastation – and is a celebration of the fact that despite the damage, and against all odds…

From the Dust, Like Doves We Rise.

Yael Farber
Oxford, UK, Premier International Performance, 2003

AMAJUBA
LIKE DOVES WE RISE

Created with and based on the lives of
Tshallo Chokwe
Roelf Matlala
Bongeka Mpongwana
Philip 'Tipo' Tindisa
Jabulile Tshabalala

This work should ideally be played on the floor to a raked audience – as opposed to on a raised stage – so that contact with the audience is immediate and dynamic. As the audience enters, there are ten large enamel bowls (five filled with water) – placed in a seemingly random fashion on the performance floor. The bowls are typical of those used in many South African homes in the townships to wash – particularly prior to running water being provided to these areas. Upstage centre is a large zinc bath – also notably of South African aesthetic – filled with dry sand, and the props the cast will use to tell their stories. Downstage left and right are two additional zinc baths. The performance area is demarcated, by lighting, as slightly smaller than the stage area. This will create a periphery along the back, left and right of the performance space, in which cast members will wait (squatting or crouching in a position of alert readiness) when not directly involved in the action. These interludes between being in the 'performance square' are never without a complete focus from each company member towards those who are presently engaged in performance – while they wait. No one leaves the stage until the conclusion of the curtain call.

Amajuba *plays without intermission.*

Each scene is linked with the South African Spirituals and Protest Songs that are and were sung in church and during the years of the struggle against Apartheid. The healing capacity of these songs should be communicated powerfully in the spirit with which each note is sung. The songs are not decorative or for effect, but rather a deep expression of emotions…an intrinsic part of the narrative of pain and resilience that Amajuba *seeks to articulate and ultimately celebrate.*

A NOTE ON THE VERNACULAR LANGUAGES

There are eleven official languages in South Africa – and several unofficial but widely used dialects and languages. The vernaculars appearing in the text are indicative of the ethnic group from which each actor hails. Generally speaking, most black South Africans speak several languages, but the stories indicate the communities the artists were raised in. The vernacular in BONGI's story is a rural Xhosa; ROELF's story reflects the Afrikaans spoken in the 'coloured' communities of Johannesburg and the Pedi of Petersburg. TIPO's story uses the Pedi and Tswana spoken in his family and Soshanguwe Township. JABU's family is Zulu – and the vernacular in her story largely reflects this, as well as the 'tsotsi-taal' (street / gangster slang) widely spoken in Soweto and the larger townships. TSHALLO's story indicates the Tswana he spoke when growing up; the street slang of Soshanguwe Township; and the mix of other dialects inevitable in the melange of those in the community and involved in the political struggle.

(A single voice in the dark sings. The company's voices rise in response. It is a call and refrain popularly sung by the young 'comrades' of the politcial struggle in South Africa, during the turbulent eighties. This refrain is repeated indefinitely during this prologue. Lights rise on five performers standing in large enamel bowls, each illuminated by a single ray of light. The effect is evocative and intimate. The song continues gently under the spoken text, which is addressed directly to the audience.)

BONGI *(With longing.)* All my life – I have waited for the moment when the future would arrive. As a girl – I knew that some day the present would be the past. And I wanted the present to pass. I wanted the past to be the past – a country I would never have to visit again. From dust we come. And to dust shall we return…

Never to pass this way again.

JABU *(Smiling gently at the memory.)* Everything was so much simpler when I was a child…like washing myself. All I had to do was sit there and let Mama and the water do the work. But things change. The train pulls out of each station – forever going forward. And home is nowhere but in your memories.

TIPO Growing up in the townships – washing was no simple matter. All we had were those small anyana [small] bowls.

And no matter how hard I tried –

I couldn't reach around to clean my back.

(With a smile and a wink.) So I decided to forget what's behind me…

And concentrate on making my front look good.

ROELF I remember the day I realised I was growing. I couldn't fit in the bowl anymore. I understood then that someday I would be a man... And washing was never going to be simple again.

But year by year – the memories gather like dust...

Until we feel we will never be clean.

(The singing swells, as the cast stand and gather the bowls of water. They maintain the song as they move the enamel bowls to the periphery of the stage – forming a border around the playing area. The cast gather centre stage. The singing continues beneath the following:)

TSHALLO We come from a time and place that we would rather forget.

We are the lost generation of our country – where everyone has a story to tell. And most would rather forget. There is nothing special about our stories – but tonight we will tell them. For somewhere beneath the dust is the past...

And until we go back and claim each broken piece – We will never be free.

(The song resolves.)

(*BONGI closes her eyes and, lifting her arms in praise, begins to sing. The company turns to watch her. They circle her and join the song. It is a ritual they will repeat, preceding each new narrative: the person about to share their 'story' will stand centre, as the others encircle him/her – singing the story's 'theme' song.*)

(*BONGI Sings*)

O Lerato – O Lerato – O Lerato*

[You are Love – You are Love – You are Love]

Morena Jesu.

[Lord Jesus.]

O Lesedi – O Lesedi – O Lesedi

[You are Light – You are Light – You are Light]

Morena Jesu.

[Lord Jesus.]

Watshepeha – Watshepeha – Watshepeha

[You are Trustworthy – You are Trustworthy – You are Trustworthy]

Morena Jesu.

[Lord Jesus.]

(*The other cast members support her by her outstretched arms, and lower her to the ground. Leaving her seated centre stage, they retreat to the shadows on the periphery. BONGI concludes her song, looks up at the audience and smiles.*)

BONGI   I grew up between two rivers in the rural Transkei. The nearest village was two hours away. If I faced the mountain – Mgqumangwe River was on my left, and Zibhiza River was on my right. As a child – I would try to see where these two rivers met and ran towards the sea. Somewhere out there – beyond my village – was a world where children had enough

---

* Lyrics from a traditional South African spiritual hymn commonly sung in church & community contexts.

to eat and a mother to hold them when they were too scared to sleep. There are so many shadows in my past that I have never spoken about. So many questions that no-one can answer today.

But sometimes – when I sing… I'm back there in Stavela Village. I can hear it – I can feel it – as if it were just yesterday.

(*Softly, they are singing a song from her childhood – transporting her back to the past.*)

Mna ndivuswe yingoma*

[I was woken by a song]

Ndivuswe yingoma

[Woken by a song]

Yatsho, ndilele phantsi

[From a deep sleep]

Yatshw' ingoma

[The song continued]

Yatsho, ndilele phansi

[From a deep sleep]

Iye yatsho lengoma

[The song went on]

Yatshw' ingoma

[It continued / It went on]

(*The other actors appear upstage of her, in a shaft of morning sun. They carry large enamel bowls on their heads – calling out to her.*)

CHILDREN   (*As though from a distance.*)
                  Bongeka! Masihambeni siyokukha amanzi.

                  [Bongeka! Let's go and fetch water.]

* Lyrics from an indigenous song from Bongi's village Stavela. Original source is unknown.

BONGI We had no running water or electricity…and as children – we would have to fetch water from the river each day.

CHILD BONGI (*In response to the other children.*)
Ndiyeza! Ningandishiyi!
[I'm coming! Don't leave me behind!]

(*She rises, balancing a bowl on the top of her head, and runs to join the other children. They are already on their way to the river – where they will gather water, as they continue to sing.*)

———————

Yatsho, ndilele phansi
[From a deep sleep]
Iye yatsho lengoma
[The song continued]
Yatsh' Ingoma
[It went on]

———

(*The children place their bowls on the river bank, and sit together in the morning sun.*)

BONGI In Stavela Village our lives were governed by hunger. Our stomachs were always empty and our heads were always light. As children – we would spend hours talking about the food we would never have. It helped fill our stomachs just to dream about food.

CHILD 1 Mna ndingada ukutya i Turkey, ne Mayonnaise!
[I'd like to eat Turkey, and Mayonnaise!]

(*The others giggle and moan with longing at the thought.*)

CHILD 2 Mna ndingathanda ukutya i Curry ne Rice!
[I'd like to eat Curry and Rice!]

(They all react by licking their lips and trying to pluck such a dish from the air.)

CHILD 3 Mna ndingathanda ukutya i Jelly ne Custard!
[I'd like to eat Jelly and Custard!]

(The excitement is growing, as they kick their legs and grab at imaginary jelly and custard.)

CHILD 4 Mna ndingathanda ukutya i ice-cream ne pudding!
[I'd like to eat ice cream and pudding!]

(They fall silent suddenly – confused by this last suggestion.)

CHILDREN Yintoni i pudding?
[What is 'pudding'?]

CHILD 4 *(Uncertain.)* I don't know… Nice things for white people!

(They explode into laughter, pointing at and teasing the initiator of this idea.)

CHILD 2 Haai! Haai! [Hey! Hey!]

(Triumphantly.) Mna ndingathanda ukutya… i Kentucky Fried!
[I'd like to eat…Kentucky Fried!]

(Triumphantly.) A BUCKET FOR TEN!

(They roar with delight.)

BONGI Sometimes we could forget our hunger – by playing for a few hours together.

(They leap into 'Pimpire' – a childhood game of intricate leg work and hand clapping. When the song is over, the other children pick up their bowls and begin to leave. Night is falling. MPUME, BONGI's older sister, calls out to one of the boys.)

MPUME   Solomzi kutheni nigoduka ngoku nje?

[Solomzi why are you going home now?]

SOLOMZI   Kufanele sigoduke.

[We have to go home.]

Our mothers are waiting for us.

MPUME   *(Waving and feigning nonchalance.)*

OK! Sakubonana ngomso ke.

[OK! See you tomorrow then.]

BONGI But that hour would always come when all the other children returned to their families at home. And Mpume, my sister, and I would stay outside as long as we could – because we had no parents or food to go home to. Our parents had abandoned us when we were children. Even in Stavela Village – we were the poorest of the poor.

(The other cast members hold the enamel bowls vertically, in front of their face, creating the closed door of each hut in the village.)

We borrowed from the neighbours – in spite of the shame.

(The sisters go door to door, asking for food and being turned away. They knock.)

NEIGHBOUR 1   *(Whispering from behind the closed 'door'.)*

Ngubani lowo?

[Who is it?]

| MPUME | Ndim uNompumelelo, Tata. |
| | [It's me Nompumelelo, Father (Term of respect).] |

| NEIGHBOUR 1 | Ufuna ntoni? |
| | [What do you want?] |

| MPUME | Tata, bendizocela imilimili. |
| | [Father, I'm here to ask for some maize meal.] |

| NEIGHBOUR 1 | Oh! I'm sorry my child. |

(*They turn away and knock on the next door.*)

| NEIGHBOUR 2 | Ngubani lowo? |
| | [Who is it?] |

| CHILD BONGI | Ndim uBongeka, Tata. |
| | [It's Bongeka, Father.] |

| NEIGHBOUR 2 | Ufuna ntoni? |
| | [What do you want?] |

| CHILD BONGI | Ubethi usisi ndizocel'iswekile, Tata. |
| | [My sister has sent me to ask for sugar, Father.] |

| NEIGHBOUR 2 | Ayikho! There's none! |

BONGI   In our village – it was not often that anyone had food to spare.

(*They knock on the next door.*)

| NEIGHBOUR 3 | I'm sorry there's nothing, mntanam [my child]. |

(*The girls turn to each other in despair. BONGI begins to cry.*)

MPUME   (*Taking charge.*) Bongeka, masikh'imifino.

[Bongeka, let's pick wild spinach.]

CHILD BONGI   Kulungile sisi.

[OK sister.]

(*They pick frantically at the ground, putting the wild spinach in a three-legged black iron pot.*)

BONGI   Hunger is an animal. It eats you slowly from the inside. Most nights we picked wild spinach and boiled it – just to stay alive.

(*They return to their house – indicated by a square of light and an upturned bath.*)

MPUME   (*Praying over the pot.*) Nkosi sikelela oku kutya. Amen.

[God bless this food. Amen]

(*They quickly devour the little there is.*)

BONGI   There was never enough. For as long as I can remember, hunger was always there…

CHILD BONGI   (*Scratching in the dry pot.*)
Sisi mna andihluthanga. Akukho ukutya okuseleyo?

[Sister! I haven't had enough. Is there any food left?]

MPUME   Hayi Bongeka, akukho. Kwaye iphelile nemali yale nyanga

[No Bongeka, there isn't. And the money for this month is finished.]

That's all we have.

CHILD BONGI   (*Clutching her stomach.*) Sisi, isisu sam...
sibuhlungu.

[Sister, my stomach...it hurts.]

MPUME   (*Holding her against the pain.*)
Oh Bongi – sukhathazeka, Sisi.

[Oh Bongi – don't worry, Sister.]

The pain will pass.

BONGI   But the pain did *not* pass. It became a part of my life.

We would go to sleep on empty stomachs...sometimes for weeks at a time.

(*She sings a few notes of 'O Lerato' communicating the pain through song.*)

O Lesedi – O Lesedi

[You are Light – You are Light]

Morena Jesu.

[Lord Jesus.]

When I recall the shadows of those years – I try hard also to remember the small moments of joy.

(*An old man, in a ragged black jacket and hat, totters through the village towards his house, singing drunkenly.*)

TATOMKHULU   (*Singing.*)

Oonomathotholo?

[The Ancestral Spirits]

Bayeza kusasa.

[Are coming tomorrow.]

Abagulayo – bayeza kusasa, bayeza.

[Those who are sick should know – they are coming tomorrow.]

YAEL FARBER & THE CAST

Bayeza kusasa.

[They are coming tomorrow.]

BONGI   (*Laughing gently at the memory.*) The sound of my grandfather returning in the evenings… Calling me to sit with him in his house next door.

     TATOMKHULU   (*Calling out, despite the late hour.*) Bongi?

     CHILD BONGI   (*Calling back.*) Tatomkhulu? [Grandfather?]

     TATOMKHULU   (*Slurring.*) Bongi! Suhlala nje yizondinceda!
                          [Bongi! Don't just sit there, come and help me!]

     (*She runs to him joyfully and helps him to stagger home, trying to quieten his song and prevent him from waking the village.*)

BONGI   (*Once in his house.*)
Tatomkhulu – jong'isitulo!
[Grandfather – mind the chair!]

     (*She tries to help him into the chair but they tumble to the floor, laughing.*)

     TATOMKHULU   Hayi maan! Andinxilanga olo hlobo!
                           [Hey man! I'm not that drunk!]

BONGI   I loved that old man! But I hardly ever saw him sober. Still he was the only father I have ever known.

     (*BONGI helps him to the chair – an upturned zinc bath – and sits at his feet tying his shoe laces.*)

CHILD BONGI	Tatomkhulu, utata kaZovuyo ubefikile ezobolek'isarha.
	[Grandfather, Zovuyo's father was here to borrow your saw.]
	He was here to borrow the saw.

TATOMKHULU	(*Slurring.*) Uh uh Bongi. Neh! Neh! Neh!!
	[No no Bongi. No! No! No!]
	Uzoyenzani?
	[What is he going to do with it?]
	Why can't he buy his own saw?

CHILD BONGI	Uthe ufuna ukwakha isibaya.
	[He said he wants to build a kraal.]

TATOMKHULU	Ye Hey Bongi? Did you ever see a saw that saws like this saw saws?

(*They laugh together.*)

CHILD BONGI	Tatomkhulu! Ndithini kutata ka Zovuyo?
	[Grandfather! What do I tell Zovuyo's father?]
	Uyavuma okanye awuvumi ngesarha?
	[Are you saying yes or no about the saw?]
	Tatomkhulu? Tatomkhulu?
	[Grandfather? Grandfather?]

(*But he is snoring softly.*

BONGI rises and tiptoes to the door, leaving him to sleep.)

(*She whispers.*) Good night, Tatomkhulu.

(*MPUME sings softly to herself from inside their house. BONGI watches her quietly.*)

BONGI I depended on my thirteen year old sister for everything. But Mpume was a child herself, and she couldn't carry us both.

(MPUME covers BONGI with a blanket as she lies in her lap. They sing together in gentle harmony.)

Under a big umbrella.*
Under a coconut tree.
Going to school together.
Waiting and waiting for you.

MPUME   *(Tentatively.)* Bongi...

CHILD BONGI   Sisi? Sister?

MPUME   *(Delicately, after a pause.)*
                 I'm going.

(BONGI turns away in shock and quietly starts to cry.)

Kufanele ndihambe ndiye esikolweni.
[I have to leave the village to start school.]
Uzakundikhapha ukuya esitishini?
[Will you walk me to the station?]

CHILD BONGI   Andithi uzondityelela, Sisi?
                 [Will you visit me, Sister?]

MPUME   *(Trying to hold back her tears.)* I'll come back
                 for you someday, Ma Bongi. I promise!

(They embrace, weeping. They rise, and walk to the station, singing and holding the ends of the blanket between them.)

Under a big umbrella.
Under a coconut tree.
Going to school together.

---

* A children's song commonly taught to pre-school and primary school children in South Africa

BONGI I walked her the two hours to the station.

(*They wave goodbye to one another and sing.*)

————————————

Waiting and waiting for you…

————————————

(*MPUME drops her end of the blanket – severing the connection between them – and disappears into the shadows.*)

BONGI And at eight years old – I was abandoned. From then on – everyone in the village knew it: In the Mpongwana house – on the outskirts of the village – there was a little girl living there on her own.

CHILD BONGI   (*Looking around anxiously, she sings.*)

————————————

Waiting and waiting for you.

————————————

(*She scratches in the pot. There is nothing in it but sand. A cloud of dust rises. She pushes the pot over in despair, and begins to weep.*

Praying desperately.)

Bawo wethu osezulwini, Maliphathwe ngobungcwele igama lakho.
[Our Father who art in heaven, Hallowed be thy name.]
Ubukumkani bakho mabufike, Intando yakho mayenziwe emhlabeni, Njengoba isenziwa ezulwini
[Thy kingdom come, Thy will be done, On earth as it is in heaven]
Siphe namhlanje isonka sethu semihla ngamihla. Usixolele izono zethu, njengoba nathi sibaxolela abo basonayo thina.

[Give us this day our daily bread. Forgive u

as we forgive those who trespass against u

Ungasingenisi ebuhendweni, usisi
enkohlakalweni.

[Lead us not into temptation, but deliver us 1 .... evil.]

Ngokuba ubukumkani bobakho, Namandla
ngawakho, nobungcwalisa bobakho

[For thine is the Kingdom, The power and the glory.]

Kude kube ngunaphakade. Amen.

[Forever and ever. Amen.]

(*A strange whispering fills the house. Frightening voices imitate her prayers and laugh amongst themselves.*)

BONGI I would hear voices in that house and see figures in the beams of the roof. I wanted to sleep to get away from the fear...but the hunger pains kept me awake.

(*The 'Mpundulus'* [Zombies] *come out of the shadows. They claw at her blanket, trying to carry her away into their world. BONGI manages to free herself from their grasping. She runs – terrified – to TATOMKHULU's door, frantically knocks and enters.*)

CHILD BONGI Tatomkhulu? Tatomkhulu?

[Grandfather? Grandfather?]

TATOMKHULU (*Drunk and singing to himself.*)
Bayeza kusasa.

[They are coming tomorrow.]

Abagulayo – bayeza kusasa, bayeza.

[Those who are sick should know – they are coming tomorrow.]

CHILD BONGI Tatomkhulu!

(*She falls at his feet, weeping.*)

Kunezinto ezihamba phezu kwendlu phaya
ekhaya.

[Granfather, there are things walking on the roof at
home.]

Tatomkhulu mna ndifuna umama.
Kutheni umama engezi kuzondilanda nje?

[Why doesn't mama come and get me? Grandfather, I
want my mother.]

I'm hungry, and I'm scared!

(*But he is asleep, snoring softly.*)

(*Backing towards the door, in despair.*) Good
night Tatomkhulu.

(*The company begins to sing 'O Lerato', stepping forward
with the bowls in front of their faces – creating the village's
closed doors. She knocks at each door – but there is no
response. She sits.*)

BONGI Night after night – I lay in the dark, praying to be heard. But
no one came for me. I lived on my own until I was old enough
to walk away. Whenever I visit Stavela Village today… I feel
nothing but despair. I lost my childhood. I lost myself. I know
I lost so much there. But how do we lose things we never had?
Why do I grieve for what was never mine? I know no one has
any answers for me today. All I have is a voice that God gave
me to sing with…and a hunger in my soul that won't go away.

(*She closes her eyes, and begins to sing – as the cast circle
her.*)

O Lesedi – O Lesedi – O Lesedi

[You are Light – You are Light – You are Light]

Morena Jesu.

[Lord Jesus].

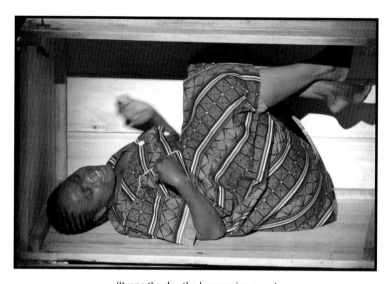

'It was the day the heavy rains came'

THEMBI MTSHALI-JONES IN **A WOMAN IN WAITING** • PHOTOGRAPHER: RICHARD DAGENAIS

'My father gave me the praises of our Ancestors'

THEMBI MTSHALI-JONES IN **A WOMAN IN WAITING** • PHOTOGRAPHER: RICHARD DAGENAIS

I

'Sabhoza: I remember all your blessings… But mostly I remember waiting'
THEMBI MTSHALI-JONES IN **A WOMAN IN WAITING** • PHOTOGRAPHER: RICHARD DAGENAIS

'Houses with toilets of such big importance… that they could swallow a woman'
THEMBI MTSHALI-JONES IN **A WOMAN IN WAITING** • PHOTOGRAPHER: RICHARD DAGENAIS

'Standing next to Mama, I would watch her sing her favourite hymn'
THEMBI MTSHALI-JONES IN **A WOMAN IN WAITING** • PHOTOGRAPHER: RICHARD DAGENAIS

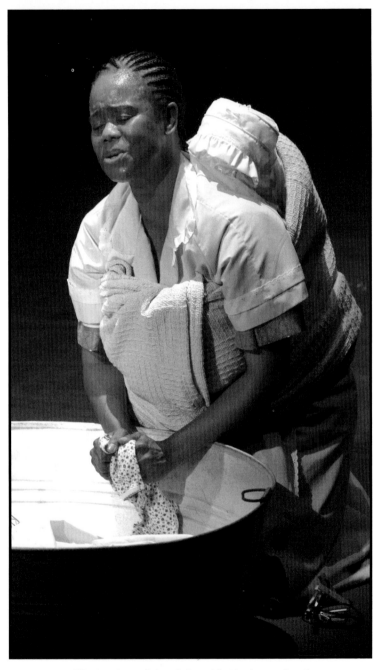

'My sister breastfed my baby, while I took care of you'

THEMBI MTSHALI-JONES IN **A WOMAN IN WAITING** • PHOTOGRAPHER: RICHARD DAGENAIS

'There is time lost that I mourn. Time I can never reclaim'
THEMBI MTSHALI-JONES IN **A WOMAN IN WAITING** • PHOTOGRAPHER: RICHARD DAGENAIS

'O, that my tongue were in the thunder's mouth'
THEMBI MTSHALI-JONES IN **A WOMAN IN WAITING** • PHOTOGRAPHER: RICHARD DAGENAIS

V

'All I have is a voice that God gave me to sing with' [FROM LEFT] TSHALLO CHOKWE, JABULILE TSHABALALA, [CENTRE] BONGEKA MPONGWANA, ROELF MATLALA, 'TIPO' TINDISA

AMAJUBA • PHOTOGRAPHER: HEIDRUN LÖHR

'He's not white! He's a Bushy!' [FROM LEFT] 'TIPO' TINDISA, ROELF MATLALA, JABULILE TSHABALALA, BONGEKA MPONGWANA

AMAJUBA • PHOTOGRAPHER: HEIDRUN LÖHR

'Keep looking over your shoulder. For the rest of your life – I will be there'

FOREGROUND: ROELF MATLALA; BACKGROUND: BONGEKA MPONGWANA

AMAJUBA • PHOTOGRAPHER: HEIDRUN LÖHR

'Why had I broken the rhythm of this family? It was supposed to be a girl.'

'TIPO' TINDISA & COMPANY IN **AMAJUBA** • PHOTOGRAPHER: ROBERT DAY

'I hated this country, where we go to more funerals than weddings in our lives'

'TIPO' TINDISA, BONGEKA MPONGWANA, ROELF MATLALA, [KNEELING] JABULILE TSHABALALA, TSHALLO CHOKWE

AMAJUBA • PHOTOGRAPHER: GENE PITTMAN

'I don't know what other people were doing at 15 years old – but we were trying to survive'.

ROELF MATLALA, 'TIPO' TINDISA, TSHALLO CHOKWE, JABULILE TSHABALALA, BONGEKA MPONGWANA

AMAJUBA • PHOTOGRAPHER: GENE PITTMAN

'If I died it didn't matter... Forward! Forward we go!'

'TIPO' TINDISA, [CENTRE] TSHALLO CHOKWE, JABULILE TSHABALALA, BONGEKA MPONGWANA

AMAJUBA • PHOTOGRAPHER: ROBERT DAY

'Those years shaped us. We were children.'
[FOREGROUND] TSHALLO CHOKWE [BACKGROUND] COMPANY
AMAJUBA • PHOTOGRAPHER: GENE PITTMAN

'We all have to stand in the rain and wash away the pain' JABULILE TSHABALALA, TSHALLO
CHOKWE, [IN BATH] 'TIPO' TINDISA, BONGEKA MPONGWANA, ROELF MATLALA
AMAJUBA • PHOTOGRAPHER: GENE PITTMAN

'And from the Dust like Doves we will Rise'
[FOREGROUND] TSHALLO CHOKWE [BACKGROUND] ROELF MATLALA
AMAJUBA • PHOTOGRAPHER: GENE PITTMAN

'When does the soul leave the body? At which precise moment?'
DUMA KUMALO IN HE LEFT QUIETLY • PHOTOGRAPHER: JOHN HOGG

'I am Duma Kumalo. Prisoner Number V-34 58'
DUMA KUMALO IN HE LEFT QUIETLY • PHOTOGRAPHER: JOHN HOGG

'There are no mirrors here. I can't see myself getting older'

LEBOHANG ELEPHANT & DUMA KUMALO IN **HE LEFT QUIETLY** • PHOTOGRAPHER: JOHN HOGG

'I am no longer a man. I hunger – like a child'

DUMA KUMALO, YANA SAKELARIS & LEBOHANG ELEPHANT

HE LEFT QUIETLY • PHOTOGRAPHER: JOHN HOGG

'And then we are sent to the Pot'

DUMA KUMALO, [CENTRE] LEBOHANG ELEPHANT, YANA SAKELARIS

HE LEFT QUIETLY • PHOTOGRAPHER: JOHN HOGG

'How many times can a man die?'

LEBOHANG ELEPHANT IN **HE LEFT QUIETLY** • PHOTOGRAPHER: JOHN HOGG

'He left quietly. That's all'
LEBOHANG ELEPHANT IN **HE LEFT QUIETLY** • PHOTOGRAPHER: JOHN HOGG

'Shoes... Worn by the forgotten men of Death Row'
DUMA KUMALO IN **HE LEFT QUIETLY** • PHOTOGRAPHER: JOHN HOGG

'This is our history. We all come from this broken place'

DUMA KUMALO & LEBOHANG ELEPHANT IN **HE LEFT QUIETLY** • PHOTOGRAPHER: JOHN HOGG

Watshepeha – Watshepeha – Watshepeha

[You are Trustworthy – You are Trustworthy – You are Trustworthy]

Morena Jesu.

[Lord Jesus.]

(*They continue to sing, as they move swiftly to set props for the next story.*)

takes his place centre stage and the cast circle him – casting long shadows and chanting ominously in a whisper.)

Boesman Kataar*

[A racist name for a bi-racial person]

Makuta-kuta tlhogo

[You can pretend to be white,

but once we shave off your hair,]

Gwasala phatlha fela!

[You will be a person, like any other!]

(The cast disperses, leaving ROELF centre stage. He looks at the audience and smiles.)

ROELF   'Amper'. [Almost.] I like that word! In Afrikaans it means 'Almost', 'Nearly…but not quite'. 'Amper' black. 'Amper' white. But neither…not quite. No matter where you go or what you do… If you are a mixed breed – you are neither here nor there. Just a 'Bushy', a 'Hotnot', a 'Boesman'. [Derogatory names for a person of mixed race] 'Amper' a Somebody…

But not quite!

(The company begins to sing an upbeat traditional 'coloured' song.)

Die son het gaan saak onder by die wingerd. Ons is baie honger†

[The sun has set, it's under the vineyard. We are very hungry.]

---

* A taunting children's rhyme commonly heard in South Africa, when children of mixed race are being teased

† A traditional Afrikaans song from the 'coloured' (bi-racial) community of South Africa

Die son het gaan saak onder by die wingerd. Ons is baie
honger

[The sun has set, it's under the vineyard. We are very hungry.]

Gee ons die 'jive' – Ons wil nou huis toe gaan.

[Give us the jive. We want to go home now.]

Gee ons die 'jive' – Ons wil nou huis toe gaan.

[Give us the jive. We want to go home now.]

(*Underscored by the song.*)

ROELF   I spent my early years living on Second Avenue – the coloured street of Alexander Township. Mama was a traditional Pedi [one of the indigenous tribes of South Africa] African Woman, and Papa's blood had some white in it.

Some say my grandmother was half Indian. And in South Africa – that made me… One-Broken-Law-after-Another!

(*The community gathers around ROELF, arguing passionately. PAPA's voice rises above the rest.*)

PAPA   He's not black! Jy is 'n [You are a] coloured.
Kyk jou hare: so soft soos silk!
[Look at your hair: As soft as silk.]
Kyk jou skin: So white soos milk!
[Look at your skin: As white as milk!]

MAMA   Ah ah Roelf! Ke nyaka o nkwe gabotse. Wena o mo pedi!
[No no Roelf! I want you to listen to me very carefully. You are a Pedi!]

NEIGHBOUR 1   Nee wat! Hy's'n 'hotnot'!
[No way! He's a 'hotnot' (derogatory term for a 'Coloured' person, derived from Hottentot – a term for the lighter-skinned Khoi-San people of the Kalahari Desert)]

NEIGHBOUR 2	Ja! Hy's 'Amper Baas'.
	[Yes! He's 'Almost Boss'! (derogatory term used to describe a 'Coloured' person as almost white enough to be an employer)]
PAPA	Jy's awright ou seun. Jy's ncaa!
	[You're alright my son. You're fine!]

ROELF My brother Solly stayed in Petersburg. He was from a different father – and *he* was as black as the night!

CHILD ROELF	(*Joking, a police officer.*) My boy, you are so dark…
	I'm going to report your blackness!
SOLLY	I may be black… But you are ugly!
CHILD ROELF	Hey Bra [brother] – I'll take ugly over black.
SOLLY	(*Wrestling with him playfully.*)
	Haaai 'Bushy-Boesman-Hotnot'!
	Hey Bushy-Bushman-Hottentot [all derogatory terms for a 'Coloured' person].
	Voetsek!
	Piss off!
	We are brothers. Finish and 'klaar' [ready].

(*They laugh and embrace.*)

ROELF There was nothing 'amper' about Solly and me. We were
brothers… Finish and 'klaar' [ready]. But when Papa left us for
good – mama started to look at me differently. She now saw in
me the half white man she loved, who had run away. She sent
me to live with my brother Solly, and my black grandmother
in Petersburg. And Jusis! [Jesus!] That's when the kak [shit] really
began…

(*A train whistles. The tin baths are pushed together and the cast gather instantly on them – creating the image and movement of a railway train and its passengers in motion.*)

It was a long train ride to get there.

(*The train whistles and everyone piles off.*)

And arriving in Petersburg... I knew then – my life would never be simple again.

(*A group of Pedi CHILDREN surround him. They are fascinated with the texture of his hair. They tentatively touch it, whispering to each other. They ask him questions, but he is shy.*)

CHILD 1   Shew! [Wow!] Your eyebrows are big!

CHILD 2   (*Touching his hair.*) And your hair is like a cat!

CHILD 3   Ke Legowa?
                 [Is he a whitey?]

CHILD 1   Ke wena mang?
                 [Who are you?]

CHILD 2   Ke eng? O simumu? Ga o itse go bua?
                 [Are you dumb? Can't you speak?]

CHILD ROELF   I don't speak Pedi! Ek praat Afrikaans. [I speak Afrikaans.]

(*They all explode into laughter.*)

ALL   Ke legowa! [He *is* a whitey!]

CHILD 3   No! He's not white!

CHILD 4	(*Gasping with realisation.*) He's a half-and-half!

CHILD 3	Jaaaaa! [Yes!] He's a 'Bushy'!

(*They dance gleefully around him, chanting.*)

CHILDREN

Boesman Kataar

[A racist name for a bi-racial person]

Makuta-kuta tlhogo

[You can pretend to be white,

but once we shave off your hair,]

Gwasala phatlha fela!

[You will be a person, like any other!]

ROELF There was no place for me here amongst the Pedi kids. And on the playground it was the Law of the Wild.

(*A group of adolescents surround him. Their manner is less amused, more threatening and aggressive.*)

BOY 1	Hey white boy! O mang? [Who are you?] What do you want here with us?

YOUNG ROELF	I stay with my granny and my brother.

BOY 2	O Legowa! [You're a whitey!] O batlang? [What do you want?] O nyakang mo ma Peding? [What do you want among us Pedis?]

YOUNG ROELF	(*Proudly.*) I'm half Pedi!

(*They all talk aggressively at once, grabbing him.*)

GIRL 1	Haai wena! [Hey you!] You are not a Pedi! You are not black!
YOUNG ROELF	Rerig! [It's true!] Go and ask my granny! I'm half Pedi!
GIRL 1	(*Ridiculing him.*) 'Half pedi! Half black!' Haai! [Hey!] Say you are a 'Bushy'!
YOUNG ROELF	Maar ek is nie 'n bushy nie! [But I'm not a 'bushy'!]
ALL	(*Pushing him brutally.*) Haai! [Hey!] Jy's 'n bushy! [You're a bushy!]

(*SOLLY is suddenly at his side. He yells and the children scatter.*)

SOLLY	Voetsek! Marago a lena! [Piss off! Or I'll kick your asses!]

ROELF Solly did what he could to protect me.

SOLLY	Sepelang! Sepelang man! [Get away! Get away, man!] Ke tla le raga marago a! [I'm going to kick the asses off you!] (*To ROELF.*) E tla kwano! [Come here!] (*With an arm around ROELF, explaining to him.*) Roelf – wena ga o tshwane le bana ba bangwe. [You don't look like the other children.] You are different!

CHILDREN	(*Following, to eavesdrop on the conversation.*) Vele! [Of course!]

SOLLY	(*Turning on them.*) SHUT UP! VOETSEK!!! [Piss off!!]

(*The children run away. SOLLY turns back to ROELF.*)

Don't look for trouble! Stay low!

You must try hard not to be noticed. Don't look people in the eye. But when shit happens…

Brother, you must fight like hell!

(*SOLLY does a spectacular spin / drop kick, winks and disappears.*)

ROELF   I tried to be invisible. I tried to stay low. But there was one person my brother could not protect me from:

(*A frightening figure of a woman rises. Her height is created by the actress standing on one of the upturned zinc baths, with an extra long skirt – creating the illusion of her towering over the children. She has a 'sjambok' – a traditional rubber whip – in her hand. She cracks the whip viciously.*)

Mrs Popo – The School Principal!

(*The school bell rings. The children gather around MRS POPO and sing with great gusto.*)

All things bright and beautiful*
All creatures great and small

* A Victorian Hymn, commonly taught and sung in South African Schools, originally written by Mrs. Cecil Frances Alexander, published in 1848

YAEL FARBER & THE CAST

All things wise and wonderful
The Lord God made them all.

(*POPO conducts the song vigorously. She cracks her whip, indicating the conclusion of the hymn. The children dash to their designated places, sitting around her in a circle. They flinch at her every move.*)

POPO   (*Smiling, but with simmering rage.*) Bantwana! [Children!] It has been reported to me – that a certain *somebody* ubedlala ibhola yentenetya apha eyadini yesikolo sam, [has been playing with a tennis ball in my schoolyard] and vandalising the school property. Now children – niyayazi into yokuba: [you know that:] I do not tolerate trespassing – especially if ndiyayazi into yokuba akukho mntwana wesikolo ofanele ukuba lapha [because we are aware that no student is permitted in that area]. But this certain… (*Her eyes fall on ROELF.*) *somebody* thinks he is too white to follow our rules. I think it's time we give him what he deserves!

(*She points her long 'sjambok' at ROELF.*)

YOUNG ROELF   Mara ga se nna, Principal! [But it wasn't me, Principal!]

POPO   Voetsek! [Piss off!] Sukundiphendula! [Don't argue with me!] You are a criminal! Nothing more! Usisikrelemnqa qha ke! [A real hard core criminal.] Mthatheni! [Stretch him!]

CHILDREN   (*Surrounding ROELF, they pull the back of his T-shirt over his head to blind him. They lift and carry him to the upturned zinc bath, chanting.*) Moyeng! Moyeng! [In the air! In the air!]

POPO   (*With sadistic enthusiasm.*) Stretch him! Stretch him!

(*The children stretch him over the zinc bath.* POPO *beats him savagely with her 'sjambok'. Then reassuming her former composure, she continues where she left off.*)

Two! Three!

(*The children continue the hymn*)

Each little flower that opens.
Each little bird that sings.
He gave them glowing colours.
He gave them tiny wings.
All things bright and beautiful
All creatures great and small.

ROELF   (*As the children continue singing,* ROELF *turns to the audience.*) I had never committed any one of the crimes Mrs Popo accused me of.

But my hair was soft and my skin was light…

And Popo the Principal hated me – for this crime alone.

(*The children conclude the hymn with a flourish.*)

CHILDREN   All things wise and wonderful
The Lord God made them all.

(*The bell rings, and the children scatter.*)

ROELF   I didn't want to go home after the beatings.

(*Whimpering,* ROELF *staggers to a private place to sit alone and cry.* SOLLY *finds him.*)

SOLLY   Roelf? What happened?

YOUNG ROELF Popo hit me again.

(SOLLY turns away, furious, and swears under his breath.)

SOLLY Eish! Wa ntena mosadi wo! Genka mo
      tshwara… Are sepele!
      [Goddamit! That woman makes me mad! If I catch her
      doing this to you… Let's go!]

(He helps his brother to walk home.)

GRANNY *(Calling for her grandsons into the darkening
      night.)* ROELF? SOLLY?

YOUNG ROELF *(Whispering as they approach the house.)*
      Asseblief Buti! [Please brother!] Don't tell
      Granny. It will only make things worse.

SOLLY OK… Sepela oyi phihla ka morago ga
      mohlare ola.
      [OK… Go and hide there behind the tree.]

GRANNY *(Calling out.)* Roelf we!

*(Night has fallen. SOLLY joins GRANDMOTHER in the
house.)*

      O kae moshimane wo?
      [Where is this boy?]

SOLLY He's coming Koko [Granny]. Just go back to
      sleep.

(ROELF sits alone outside, crying. The cast sing gently.)

All creatures great and small.
All things wise and wonderful.
The Lord God made them all.

(The school bell rings. It is daytime and the children are playing a game in the school yard.)

CHILDREN   *(Chanting the game's rhyme.)* Tsotsi! Kwela Kwela!

[Gangster / Criminal! Get on the van!]

ROELF   As time passed – the children started to accept me in their own way.

CHILD   Hey 'half-and-half'… Come and play!

(He leaps up eagerly and joins the others.)

CHILDREN   Tsotsi! Kwela Kwela!

(He gleefully joins them – but makes a mistake in the complex footwork of the game. They all immediately start to yell at him.)

ROELF   But hostility and trouble were never far away.

CHILDREN   *(Shoving him between them.)*
Bushy! Boesman! [Bushman!] Hotnot! [Hottentot!]
Legowa! [Whitey!] Amper baas! [Almost boss!]
Kleurling! [Coloured!] PAUL KRUGER'S CHILD!!!
[Paul Kruger: a conservative, white, Afrikaans past
President of South Africa – was 'scandalously'
rumoured to have fathered a child with a black
woman.]

(They push him to the ground.)

ROELF   And Mrs Popo never missed an opportunity to beat me.

(The children gather around ROELF and inform him with glee.)

CHILD	Heyi wena Tsotsi!
	[Hey you criminal!]
	Mrs Popo wants you in her office…

| CHILDREN | NOW!!!!!! |

(*They scatter – giggling.*)

ROELF   I would dream about Mrs Popo every night… especially during school holidays.

> (*POPO strides out of the shadows. Her height is created by the actress sitting on the shoulders of an actor – hidden beneath her extra-long skirt. The other cast members sing a haunting refrain to create the terror of the nightmare.*)

POPO	Hey wena Tsotsi!
	[Hey you criminal!]
	Uphi unyoko?
	[Where is your mother?]
	Uphi uyihlo?
	[Where is your father?]
	Kutheni ungayi kuyohlala namanye amalawu nje?
	[Why aren't you with other Coloureds?]
	Why are you not with the other half breeds?
	You make me sick! Keep looking over your shoulder.
	For the rest of your life… I will be there!

(*She retreats back into the shadows.*)

ROELF   In all the years Popo beat me – she never knew my name.

CHILDREN	(*Chanting and dancing in the rain.*)
	Mma mpulele!
	Mother open for me!

Pula Yana!

It is raining!

Mma mpulele!

Mother open for me!

Pula Yana!

It is raining!

(*The children are frolicking in the rain.*)

ROELF   One night during school holidays – it rained very hard. And the next morning – the children were going swimming because the river was full.

SOLLY   Roelf – C'mon! Let's go swim!

YOUNG ROELF   (*Anxiously.*) I can't Solly! There will be children there who don't know me.

SOLLY   Don't worry Bra! [Brother!] I'll protect you. Come on!

(*ROELF runs excitedly to the river, following the other children. The cast creates a river with their arms, holding one of the actors airborne horizontally – to create the illusion that he is swimming.*)

SWIMMING BOY   Hey Boesman! Don't be scared! Come and swim!

ROELF   I couldn't see Solly anywhere. But I decided to take the plunge.

(*He dives in and swims.*)

But suddenly… (*Glancing over his shoulder.*) two boys were coming for me! (*They are suddenly upon him.*)

BOYS   Hey Boesman! You're going to drown!

(*Laughing, they push him repeatedly beneath the water. Suddenly SOLLY is upon them. He fights the boys off and pulls ROELF, sputtering and coughing, from the water.*)

SOLLY U Sharp? [Are you alright?]

YOUNG ROELF (*Gasping for breath, he points to his injured leg.*) My knee!!!

SOLLY puts ROELF on his back and carries him home.

GRANNY (*Horrified.*) What happened?

SOLLY Koko! [Granny!] Some children tried to drown him! They hurt his knee.

GRANNY Awa lemala? [Are you hurt?]

YOUNG ROELF Ke gobetse, Koko. [Yes I'm hurt, Granny.] Mo! [Here!] (*Pointing to his knee.*)

GRANNY (*Furious.*) Ba tlo nyela dintja tse!
[They'll shit themselves – those bloody dogs!]
(*Turning on SOLLY.*) But Solly – where were you?
I told you to look after your brother!

SOLLY I tried Koko! [Granny!]

YOUNG ROELF O maaka! [You are lying!]

(*Distraught.*) I couldn't see you Solly! You left me there!

SOLLY	(*Suddenly exploding – he grabs* ROELF *violently.*) Wa ntapisa! [I'm tired of you!] It's not my fault the other kids hate you! You are not the only one who is suffering here! You are NOT my brother! Fokkin' [fucking] half breed!
YOUNG ROELF	Solly please…
SOLLY	(*He turns to go – but stops for a moment – filled with regret.*) I'm sorry! (*But he knows the damage is done. He leaves.*)
ROELF	(*Calling after him frantically.*) Solly please! Come back! But he was gone!

(*The children gather around* MRS POPO, *chanting their Multiplication Tables in unison.*)

CHILDREN	One times two equals two Two times two equals four Three times two equals six Four times two equals eight

ROELF I stayed away from school for three months because of my injured knee. But soon…Popo sent for me!

(ROELF *arrives on crutches.* MRS POPO *turns to the class with a sneer.*)

POPO	A certain *somebody* has been *pretending* to be injured, and has missed three months of

school! He must be taught a lesson! What do you say? Shall we give him what he deserves.

YOUNG ROELF   (*Panicking.*) But – but Teacher... Some boys...they tried to drown me. Look! I can't straighten my knee!

POPO   (*With relish.*) Ja! [Yes!] Let us help him straighten his knee! Stretch him!

(*He screams as the children stretch him over the zinc bath, wrenching his injured knee. POPO whips him brutally, as the children sing.*)

All things bright and beautiful
All creatures great and small
All things wise and wonderful
The Lord God made them all.

(*ROELF stands and recomposes himself.*)

ROELF   For the rest of my school years – every day – Mrs Popo beat me. To this day – she owns something inside me that I am still trying to set free.

(*Smiling with resignation.*) Amper [almost] black, amper white.

Almost a somebody... But not quite!

(*The others chant in an ominous whisper, circling him.*)

Boesman Kataar...

[A racist name for a bi-racial person]

Makuta-kuta tlhogo...

[You can pretend to be white,

But once we shave off your hair,]

Gwasala phatlha fela!

[You will be a person, like any other!]

(*ROELF stands centre as the shadowy figures surround him from his past. Suddenly they peel off and the cast begins to set up for the next story. Small, slim and fast on his feet – TIPO suddenly breaks from the group and starts to run.*)

(TIPO slips with ease between the grasping hands of the cast members who chase him relentlessly. As he runs – the cast sings.)

Njalo, njalo, njalo*

[Always, always, always]

Siya thandaza, siyanikela

[We pray, we offer]

Siya dumisa, njalo

[We praise Him, always.]

(TIPO looks around anxiously, and comes to sit on the upturned tin bath. He takes a moment to catch his breath, and then looks up at the audience. He is the 'joker' of the cast – always ready with a mischievous smile and a twinkle in his eye.)

TIPO 'Ke letebele lekwakwanyawe Ke Tlou letebele ke lebabatlang.'

[I am the Ndebele. I am the elephant. I walk tall. I am everywhere.]

That's how my father used to praise me. 'Mojalefa' [Heir].

'My last born.' That's what my mother said.

But I am NOT the last born. It was just a position allocated to me by my family.

It was A Girl – A Boy – A Girl – A Boy… A BOY… A Girl.

(As TIPO calls out his brothers' and sisters' arrivals in the family, the cast line up with their backs to the audience. TIPO takes his place in the line, according to his chronology in the family. He faces the audience.)

* Lyrics from a traditional South African spiritual hymn commonly sung in church & community contexts.

'Why me?' I used to ask myself again and again: 'Why me? Why have I broken the rhythm of this family?' It was supposed to be a girl.

Mama said...

MOTHER   (*Turning to* TIPO.) Phillip [Tipo's Christian name], ke wena mojalefa o tla re hlokomela gare godile!

[Philip, you are the heir. You will look after us in our old age.]

TIPO   Papa said...

FATHER   (*Turning to* TIPO.) Letebele ga go bohlokwa gore o ngwana wa bokae, se se bohlokwa ke gore o kgethilwe go ba mojalefa.

[It doesn't matter what number you are! You have been chosen to be the heir.]

TIPO   The duty of the last born is to take care of his parents. For most of my life I have been preparing for this job. Making sure my love is divided equally between them. Even when I was a child – I was not interested in playing with other children.

(*The other kids are playing with a ball. They call* TIPO *to join them. He does so reluctantly – but returns to his parents as soon as he can. He is happiest sitting between them.*)

MOTHER   (*Tickling him to chase him away.*)
Tsamaya o yilo tshameka le bana ba bangwe!

[Go and play with the other kids!]

(*Reluctantly, he returns to play with the others. They tease him, and chase him off.*)

SELINA   Haai! [Hey!] You are just a Mama's Baby!

(He runs away laughing – and turns to face the audience.)

TIPO We were happy in Garankuwa. Papa was Chairman of the Church – so we had to be exemplary.

> *(They create the long family table, by pushing the two zinc baths together and spreading a lace cloth over them. As they do this, the cast joyously sings.)*

Lehodimo lea sebeletswa*

[To be a child of God]

Halala!

[Exclamation, expressing joy]

Lea sebeletswa!

[Is a privilege to work hard for!]

(They gather around the table and sit.)

TIPO We prayed together...

FAMILY Ka leina la Ntate, le la Morwa, le la Moya o galalelang. Amen.

[In the name of the Father, the Son, and the Holy Spirit. Amen.]

TIPO We ate together…

(They all grab for food – but FATHER scolds them.)

FATHER Re kaseje re sa felela mo tafuleng! Le a kwishisha?

[We won't start to eat until everyone is at the table! Is that clear?]

* Lyrics from a traditional South African spiritual hymn commonly sung in church & community contexts.

TIPO We worked together.

(*They each perform their chores in the home, singing.*)

Lehodimo lea sebeletswa

[To be a child of God]

Halala!

[Exclamation, expressing joy]

Lea sebeletswa!

[Is a privledge to work hard for!]

TIPO But things changed when we received a letter from the Government Office.

FATHER   (*Holding the letter.*) Bana... [Children...]

(*The family quickly gathers around him.*)

                      (*Reading the letter.*)
Re tshwanetse go thothela Soshanguve!
[They are moving us to Soshanguve!]
They are moving us to Soshanguve!

FAMILY   (*Confused.*) Soshanguve?

THABO   Why Papa?

FATHER   The Law says: Everyone who is not a MoTswana must move out of Garangkwa.

THABO   Mara [but] Papa, this is our home!

TIPO & SISTER Hai! Aretsamayi Papa!
[No! We are not going, Father!]

FATHER   The Law is the Law.

(*Trying to look on the bright side.*)

Le se tshwenyege bana baka.

[Don't worry my children!]

Go tloba le motlakase le meetse ka ntlong…

[In the house there will be electricity, water…]

Even the toilet is going to be inside the house!

(*They shout for joy.*)

TIPO   I didn't understand that these were Forced Removals. I was excited to go. We were going to be like white people in town!

(*They pick up baths and blankets, and relocate to Soshanguwe, as the song rises.*)

Lehodimo lea sebeletswa

[To be a child of God]

Halala!

[Exclamation, expressing joy]

Lea sebeletswa!

[Is a privilege to work hard for!]

(*Arriving at their newly allocated home.*)

TIPO   This was a home where my parents could grow old in together.

(*Despite the drab nature of the government-issue house, they are all trying to be positive. FATHER, however, is distracted*).

CHILD TIPO   (*Excited.*) Wa etse keng Mama, yona inyaka fela paving.

[You know what mum – it only needs paving!]

SELINA   (*Adding her ideas.*) Ee Mama! [Yes Mom!] Ene Mama – [And Mom –] We can put big windows!

MOTHER	Ee Selina! [Yes Selina!]
CHILDREN	JA! [YES!]
MOTHER	(*To FATHER.*) Akere Zef? Zef... Zef? [Isn't it Zef? Zef...]
CHILDREN	PAPA!
FATHER	(*Startled out of his distracted mood.*) Huh? Mh hm! Yes, the toilet...very nice.

TIPO (*Turning to the audience.*) Maybe Papa had made up his mind to leave us long ago. Maybe families are not meant to be put under such pressure by relocating. I don't know who is to blame! All I know is...when we left Garankuwa, a part of my father stayed there. He would spend weekends there – and less and less time with us in Soshanguwe.

> (*MOTHER and FATHER begin to argue. The children listen quietly.*)

MOTHER	Zef, akomputse – onyakang koa Garankuwa? [Tell me Zef – what were you doing there in Garankuwa?]
FATHER	Ne keile lehung. [I was at a funeral.]
MOTHER	Aowa Zef! Funeral, beke le beke. [No Zef! Funeral, week after week.]
FATHER	(*Threatening.*) Dimakatso [Her name]... Dimakatso!
MOTHER	Ompaletsi Zef. [I give up Zef.] (*She storms off.*)

PHILIP! (*She calls for* TIPO.)

TIPO (*To the audience.*) I did what I could to keep my family together.

YOUNG TIPO (*Racing to her.*) Mama?

MAMA Ditlhako tsaka ko shoe maker!
[Go collect my shoes at the shoe maker!]

(*TIPO runs enthusiastically to do as he is asked.*)

FATHER PHILIP!

YOUNG TIPO (*Racing to his father.*) Papa?

FATHER Tsamo reka tekete.
[Go and buy me a bus ticket.]

(*TIPO runs to do as asked, but is again interrupted.*)

MOTHER PHILIP!

YOUNG TIPO (*Running to* MOTHER.) Mama?

MOTHER O ile ko Mma Moloi.
[Did you go to Mama Moloi.]

(*He dashes off.*)

FATHER PHILIP! (*TIPO runs to his father.*)
Tsama lata dry clean.
[Go and collect my dry cleaning.]

MOTHER PHILIP! (*With increasing impatience.*)

(*He runs frantically between them, trying to keep them both happy.*)

YOUNG TIPO   Mama?

MOTHER   Nkele ko societing!
                  [Go to the Society! (Social Club)]

YOUNG TIPO   Maar Mama… (*Protesting.*)
                  [But Mama…]

(*She takes off her shoe, threatening to beat him. He runs off to do as he is told.*)

FATHER   PHILIP!

YOUNG TIPO   Papa? (*He runs to FATHER – but finds him no longer there.*) Papa? (*Looking around, bewildered.*) PAPA?

(*But his FATHER is gone.*)

TIPO (*Turning to the audience.*) We lost my father bit by bit.

That's how he left us – bit by bit. He would leave for work in the mornings with a plastic bag full of things…

FATHER   (*Holding a large, full plastic bag, he doffs his hat as he leaves for work.*) Gabotse Bana.
                  [Goodbye children.]

CHILDREN   Gabotse Papa! Goodbye Papa.

(*Once out of sight, FATHER empties the contents of the plastic bag, and returns to the house.*)

YAEL FARBER & THE CAST

TIPO But when he came home in the evenings – the plastic bag was empty.

FATHER (*Returning, the empty bag is rolled up and under his arm.*) Thobela Bana. [Greetings children.]

CHILDREN Thobela Papa. [Greetings Papa.]

FATHER (*Doffing his hat to his wife.*) Dimakatso…

MOTHER Zef…

He stops in his tracks.

E kaye plastic e o tsamai leng ka yona?
[Where are the things that were in the plastic bag?]

FATHER (*Grappling for words.*) Er…ah…dry cleaners!

MOTHER (*Clicking her tongue in disapproval.*) Ja! [Yes!]

(*She flicks the bag in his face. He slinks off, sheepishly.*)

TIPO Now I understand… He was packing his things – piece by piece… Until he removed the last part of himself from our lives.

FATHER Bana… [Children…]

CHILDREN (*Gathering around him eagerly.*) Papa?

FATHER (*After a beat.*) Ka sepela! [I'm leaving!]

(*They all look at one another, bewildered.*)

Thabo…

(*He awkwardly offers his eldest son a few coins. THABO turns away in disgust.*)

Selina…

(*He offers his daughter the coins. She gratefully accepts them.*)

SELINA   (*Unsure as to what is happening.*) Bye bye
                Papa!

FATHER   Philip…

(*TIPO turns away, overcome. FATHER hastily gathers his remaining bags. As he leans over, his hat drops to the ground.*)

YOUNG TIPO   (*With great pain.*) Papa?

(*TIPO looks from MOTHER to FATHER – torn between them. FATHER hesitates for a moment, but when TIPO turns back – he is gone. Only his hat remains where he once stood.*)

(*The others sing gently.*)

Njalo, njalo, njalo

[Always, always, always]

Siya thandaza, siya nikela, Siya dumisa! Njalo

[We pray, we offer, we praise Him! Always]

TIPO (*Picking up FATHER's hat.*) So here we were in Soshanguwe – a new home, with the gap where my father used to be. (*He places FATHER's hat at his feet and looks at it.*) My father worked for Saleshouse [generic South African clothing department store].

We had always looked 'sharp' [good, fine] – dressed in style. Suddenly all those things were gone. So was the money. My mother needed to raise six children alone.

But I learned to survive... (*Winking.*)

I'm small and fast. No one can catch me.

> (*The following is a stylised sequence of movements, depicting TIPO greeting a collage of people in his community, who are asking how he is. His bravado and efforts to pretend that all is well are high spirited, poignant and increasingly frantic.*)

YOUNG TIPO   Bra Solly. KeSharp! [Brother Solly. I'm fine!]

> (*He turns and waves.*)

Ous sister Meisie! I'm fine!

> (*He turns.*)

Lerato! [Girl's name] KeSharp! [I'm 'sharp' (fine).]

> (*He turns.*)

Ke sharp man! Ke sharp! [I'm fine! I'm fine!]
Ek is ncaa! [I'm great!]

> (*His MOTHER watches him with concern.*)

MOTHER   Philip!

> (*He stops.*)

TIPO The only person I couldn't run from...was my mother.

YOUNG TIPO   Mama? (*He goes to sit beside her.*)

MOTHER   Molato Ke eng? [What's the matter?]

YOUNG TIPO   (*Avoiding her eye.*) Ah Ma... Ke sharp!
[Ah Ma... I'm fine.]

> (*She turns him to face her, and looks him in the eye.*)

MOTHER   Ha o sharp! Ke eng?
          [You are not alright! What is it?]

YOUNG TIPO   (*He breaks down, dropping his bravado.*)
              Nna mama ke mis-a Papa.
              [Ma, I miss Papa.]

MOTHER   (*Gently.*) I miss him too. Mara [But] Philip, my
          boy…

          (*Taking him squarely by the shoulders.*)

YOUNG TIPO   (*Meeting her eye.*) Mama?

MOTHER   Ngwana'ka, Tshwanetse re ithute gore batho
          bao rebaratang, ba re sia.
          [But Philip my child, we must teach ourselves that those
          we love can leave us.]
          We've got to move on! OK boy?

YOUNG TIPO   Eya Mama! [Yes Mama!]

MOTHER   A re rapeleng, bana.
          [Let us pray, children.]

ALL   (*Crossing themselves.*) Ka leina la Ntate le la
          Morwa, le la Moya o galalelang. Amen.
          [In the name of the Father, the Son, and the Holy Spirit
          Amen.]

TIPO That's when I saw how strong my mother really is. She filled
      that empty space in our new home.

MOTHER   Philip, Selina, Thabo…

YOUNG TIPO   Ma?

| MOTHER | E tla o thuse! [Come and help!] |

(*MOTHER gives orders to the children to organise the house. They sing as they work.*)

CHILDREN	Lehodimo lea sebeletswa
	[To be a child of God]
	Halala!
	[Exclamation, expressing joy]
	Lea sebeletswa!
	[Is a privilege to work hard for!]

(*They once again create the table around which they gathered as a family when FATHER was with them. This time, however, MOTHER takes her place at the head of the table.*)

| FAMILY | (*Crossing themselves.*) Ka leina la Ntate, le la Morwa, le la Moya o galalelang Amen. |
| | [In the name of the Father, the Son, and the Holy Spirit. Amen.] |

TIPO She joined a new church.

(*MOTHER sings joyously – dancing and finding her feet once again.*)

MOTHER

Lehodimo lea sebeletswa!

[Heaven is worked for!]

Halala!

[Exclamation, expressing joy]

Lea sebeletswa!

[It is worked hard for!]

TIPO She finally accepted that my father was never coming back
      – and filed for a divorce.

MOTHER   Halala!

          (*MOTHER picks up FATHER's hat from the floor. The family
          dances in celebration as the song swells. Suddenly FATHER
          comes storming in – divorce papers in hand.*)

FATHER   (*Furious.*) Dimakatso! Keng seo o seatsang.
             [What the hell are you doing?]

MOTHER   Keng kang? [What?]

FATHER   Ke ntlo yaka e!
             [This is *my* house!]
             Dis my huis! Dis my kinders!
             [This is my house! These are my children!]

MOTHER   O se mpotse ditshila.
             [Don't you talk shit to me!]

FATHER   Le wena o mpotsa ditshila.
             [It is *you* who are talking shit to *me*!]

          (*MOTHER taps FATHER's hat back onto his head – and
          points to the door.*)

             (*Incensed.*) O roga Dimakatso mo roga ke go
             betsa.
             [I will beat you, Dimakatso.]

MOTHER   Mphethe? Mphete! Mphete!
             [Hit me? Hit me then! Hit me!]

          (*FATHER moves to strike her – but suddenly TIPO and his
          brother are in front of their MOTHER – shielding her and*

YAEL FARBER & THE CAST

squaring up against their FATHER. FATHER is shocked,
humiliated. The sons he left are now men, willing and able
to defend their mother. He backs away, staring at his sons —
who hold his gaze. He turns and strides out of the house.)

TIPO I wanted to run after him like I did when I was a child – but this time, I wanted answers!

> (*TIPO begins to chase after his father. They run in intricate circles around the stage – as though through back streets and alleys.*)

YOUNG TIPO (*Realising FATHER has slipped away again, he screams.*) Papaaaaa!

TIPO But he was gone! So I just kept running.

> (*He takes off again – running and dodging as others try to interact with him. He shakes each of them off, fleeing.*)

MOTHER Philip! O e tsang ko ntlong ela?
[Philip! What are you doing in that house?]
Ka yetse gore gona le ma Comrades
[I know there are Comrades (Political Activists) there]
– and one day, my boy – they will come for you!

> (*He breaks from her and runs.*)

GIRL Philip – (*She pulls him towards her, kissing him sensuously.*)
Kade ngikulindile, bowukuphi?
[I have been waiting so long for you, where were you?]
Philip – I love you!

> (*He almost succumbs, but suddenly breaks free – and flees*).

RIEND   (*Putting an arm around him.*) Philip, a se
bioscope.
[Philip, let's go to a movie sometime.]

YOUNG TIPO   (*Peeling away.*) Uh uh. Ke Sharp!
[No. I'm fine!]

(*He runs.*)

TIPO (*Coming to a stop, he turns to the audience.*) I did a lot of
running in the years that followed. Most of us did in the
townships – during the school boycotts, consumer boycotts,
and stay-aways! Pretoria North Riot Squad would come – and
we didn't have a choice! We ran!

(*The cast vocally create the ominous sound of the throbbing
sirens signalling the approach of the notorious Pretoria North
Riot Squad. They run frantically in different directions.*)

Even if you made it home, there was nowhere to hide.

(*He dives beneath a zinc bath, concealing himself. The
POLICE knock violently on the top of the bath. He slips out
from beneath it and runs.*)

POLICE   (*Giving chase.*) Hey! Vat hom! [Get him!]
(*Calling after him.*) Ons gaan jou kry – jou
hond! [We'll get you – you dog!]

(*He runs frantically without looking back. Once safe, he
turns to look at the audience. The others join him – staring
out with haunted eyes.*)

TIPO We saw things in those years that kids shouldn't see.

There are things you never forget… But I learnt to survive!

(*He shrugs, winks and smiles.*)

YAEL FARBER & THE CAST

I run...
I hide!

(*He greets people in a stylised manner – as previously. He moves deftly from one interaction to another – reassuring everyone that he is fine, as the others sing.*)

Njalo, njalo, njalo
[Always, always, always]
Siya thandaza, siya nikela, Siya dumisa! Njalo
[We pray, we offer, we praise Him! Always]

TIPO   Bra Solly. Ke Sharp! [Brother Solly. I'm fine.]

(*He turns and waves.*) Ous sister Meisie! I'm fine! (*He turns.*)

Lerato! Ke Sharp! [I'm fine.] (*He turns.*)
Ke sharp man! Ke sharp! I'm fine!

(*He falls silent as the others sing, dancing in a circle around him.*)

FOUR • JABULILE

(*The cast retreats to the periphery. A blanket is spread centre stage. JABU goes to it and gently lies down. The others sing a slow evocative call and refrain.*)

---

uYingcwele Baba – uYingcwele.*

[You are holy my Lord – You are holy.]

uYingcwele Baba – uYingcwele.

[You are holy my Lord – You are holy.]

uYingcwele Baba – uYingcwele.

[You are holy my Lord – You are holy]

(*JABU lies sleeping on the blanket. The figure of a young boy appears near her in a shaft of light. His T-shirt is white, glowing in the light – but his face is shadowed. It is BULLY, her cousin, calling her name in a dream. She sits up into the dream. They have a soft conversation. The singing underscores the following.*)

JABU (*Astonished to see him.*) Bully? Wuwena mfanam?

[Bully? Is it you boy?]

U alright, boy?

[Are you alright, boy?]

(*BULLY gently nods his head.*)

(*Touching the back of her head.*)
Sinjani isiva? Sipholile?

[How is the scar? Has it healed?]

(*Slowly his hands grasp the bottom of his T-shirt and begin to pull and twist the fabric. He turns in the T-shirt, as though he wants to remove it but cannot. His struggle intensifies, and in the shaft of light, the white fabric creates a blur of movement. The singing of the cast grows increasingly, as do*

---

* Lyrics from a traditional South African spiritual hymn commonly sung in church & community contexts.

YAEL FARBER & THE CAST

BULLY's desperate pleas to JABU. The dream is fast becoming a nightmare.)

BULLY   Jabu… Jabu help me! Help me to undress!
               Siza ungikhumule! [Help me to undress!]
               Nceda undikhumle, Jabu! [Help me to undress, Jabu!]
               Please Jabu… Help me to undress and let me go!

JABU   Ungakhumuli boy! Ungakhumuli!
               [Don't undress boy! Don't undress!]
               Ungakhumuli boy!
               [Don't undress boy!]
               Ungakhumli!
               [Don't undress! Please!]

BULLY   *(Getting more desperate.)*
               Help me Jabu! I have to go now.
               Help me Jabu. Nceda undikhumule! [Help me to undress!]
               Nceda undikhumule, Jabu! [Help me to undress, Jabu!]
               Please Jabu. Help me! Please…

JABU *(She is lying down again, turning and muttering in her sleep.)*
               Don't… Please boy! Ungakhumuli! [Don't undress!]

BULLY   *(Calling with final despair as lights fade on him.)* Jabuuuuuuuu…

               (She wakes with a start. Everything is quiet. She realizes she has been dreaming and exhales with relief. Smiling sadly, she looks up at the audience.)

JABU   What is it to dream of the dead? Is it our longing that calls
       them? … Our grief that draws them out of the shadows late
       at night, back into our world. Or are *they* longing for *us*?
       …asking something from us that we cannot give, because to
       do so would be to let them go – forever.

           (*The cast sing a lilting childhood nursery rhyme.*)

Dikuku – Di wela Molewatle,*
[The hens – fall into the sea]
Ga difufa – Diwela Molewatle.
[When they fly – they fall into the sea]
Banna – Barweli Dilepe
[The men – are carrying axes]
Libasadi – Barweli di ngwana
[And the women – are carrying calabashes]
Bafita – Barweli rweli rweli,
[They all pass by carrying something]
Bafita – Barweli rweli rweli
[They all pass by – carrying something]

       (*BULLY's voice is suddenly that of a young boy, calling
       JABU's name. She laughs, as she recalls a time passed. The
       characters will enter the playing space as she mentions them
       – conjuring the memory of each family member. The nursery
       rhyme underscores the following.*)

BULLY   (*A young boy, pushing an imaginary toy car
                   made of wire, circles JABU.*)
                   Jabuuu? Jabuuu?

JABU   I grew up in an intimate family. It was my cousin Bully…

BULLY   Jabu – Jabu! Woza sizodlala!
                   [Jabu – Jabu! Come let's play!]

       * Indigenous children's nursery rhyme

JABU   My Uncle Pappie...

PAPPIE   (*Enter* PAPPIE – *a young man in his early
                 twenties with a gruff voice and tough
                 demeanour.*)
                 Hhe, Jabu! Wena usuyazi thithiveyitha.
                 Sowuyajola! Kulamalanga?
                 [Hey Jabu! These days you like beautifying yourself. You
                 in love?]

(*She laughs at* PAPPIE*'s playful teasing.*)

JABU   My grandmother...

GRANNY   (*A bent old woman, reprimanding* PAPPIE.)
                 Hey! Pappi bamba kahle leyo sofa.
                 Ngayithenga ngo 1964.
                 [Pappi, handle that sofa with care! I bought it in 1964!]

JABU   And myself. We were all so close. I didn't share a mother's
       breast with Pappie nor Bully. But they were my brothers.

BULLY   Jabu, woza sizodlala leyana yokushay'izandla.
                 [Jabu, come let's play that one with the clapping.]

YOUNG JABU   Konje ithini? [How does it go again?]

                 Oh ja! [Oh yes!!] (*Remembering the game.*)

(*They sing the below song, accompanied by intricate hand
clapping.*)

BULLY / JABU   Katsamaya ma... Iye mh hm! *
                 [I walked with... i-yeah mh mh!]

* Indigenous South African rhyme that accompanies a game of hand
clapping rythms.

AMAJUBA: LIKE DOVES WE RISE   151

Le bo nkgono ma… Iye mh mh!

[Old ladies… i-yeah mh – hm!]

Ba babedi ma… Iye mh mh!

[There were two of them… i-yeah mh hm!]

Ba mpotsa ma… Iye mh mh!

[They asked me … i-yeah mh hm!]

Gore keya kae… Iye mh mh!

[Where I was going… i-yeah mh hm!]

Ma botho botho! [Softy Softy!]

Ma botho botho! [Softy Softy!]

(*PAPPIE sneaks up behind them and gives BULLY a clip on the ear. BULLY runs away in tears.*)

PAPPIE   (*Yelling at JABU.*) Nibanga umsindo!

[You are making a noise!]

GRANNY   We Pappiei! Yindaba ushay'iingane?
Ungazongihlanyisa, maan!

[Pappiei! Why are you hitting the kids? Don't make me crazy, man!]

YOUNG JABU   Ungamshayi, usile! [Don't hit him, silly man!]

(*She runs to comfort BULLY.*)

BULLY   Ungishayelani? Ungangishayi!

[Why is he hitting me? Don't hit me!]

YOUNG JABU   Ukushaye kabuhlungu? [Did he hurt you?]

(*BULLY nods. JABU rubs BULLY's head where he was struck. She becomes tearful.*)

Thul'ungakhali, Bully. [Don't cry, Bully.]

JABU Whenever Bully got hurt… I would cry too. I alw
      pain like it was my own.

> (*Night has fallen. GRANNY sings an old lullaby.*)

GRANNY Thula, thula mntwana. Thula sana
        [Hush – hush child. Hush baby.]
        Thul'u mam'uzobuya ekuseni
        [Hush, Mommy will be back by morning]
        Thula sthandwa sami
        [Hush my darling]
        Thula, dudu wami.
        [Hush, sleep my sweetie.]
        Thula sthandwa
        [Hush darling]
        Sentliziyo yam
        [My dearest one]

> (*The lullaby underscores the following.*)

JABU I remember – I could not fall asleep without sucking my
      thumb and squeezing my Grandmother's breast. So, I would
      go look for her and, late at night, I would find her in the
      kitchen by the coal stove.

> (*JABU sits at GRANNY's knee with her head on GRANNY's lap,
> sucking her thumb. BULLY immediately follows, competing
> for GRANNY's affections. JABU pushes him away, and they
> are soon in a tussle.*)

Bully would join us, and we would fight until we were drowsy.
Bully always wanted half of everything I had, and eventually I
would give in.

(*She embraces him.*) What could I do? I loved him.

> (*GRANNY ushers the children onto the blanket to sleep, and
> watches them for a while in the dark. She sighs deeply and*

...es away to the shadows, leaving JABU on the blanket ...en PAPPIE and BULLY. The two stand slowly and circle ... – whispering her name. She is dreaming. The cast ... sing softly.)

---

uYingcwele Baba

[You are holy my Lord.]

uYingcwele.

[You are holy.]

PAPPIE & BULLY   (*Whispering.*) Jabu? Jabu! Wake up Jabu! We have to go.

(*JABU sits up as PAPPIE and BULLY disappear into the dark.*)

JABU   They say the dead visit us in our dreams. They come back to remind us. But daylight always comes... And I must return to a world without them. There are memories I could get lost in – like when we were all still children. But time moves. You don't stay children for long.

(*Throwing the blanket to a cast member, banishing the childhood years.*)

Not in Zola, Soweto!

(*'Kwaito' – a South African form of House Music – suddenly booms through the auditorium. JABU dances on the top of the upturned zinc bath, as the other performers dance around her. A fight breaks out amongst the men. They scream abuse and chase one another. We are on the streets of Zola, Soweto.*)

Zola! One of the most notorious locations in Soweto. Ha! Bathi kwamshay'azafe! [Ha! Where they will beat a person to death!] Where they'll stab you to death for a can of beer! In Zola you learn so many things. You learn to love! You learn to hate! You learn to protect yourself.

(*Several 'tsotsis'* [gangsters] *are suddenly circling her.*)

Things were changing. Suddenly, amajita guys were noticing me. My body was changing, inviting trouble I could not control.

(*They gather around her like wolves, whistling their approval. The gang leader – MADIBA – is particularly taken with the 13 year-old JABU.*)

TSOTSI 1   Cha cha cha!

MADIBA   Hello sweetheart.

                Ayi-baby, u-fit. [Hey baby, you look good.]

(*He is standing too close. The situation is dangerous.*)

                Awungitshele Sweetheart, ngikushayele nini I-round?
                [Tell me Sweetheart, when should I come by your place to see you?]

YOUNG JABU   Mina? [Me?]

MADIBA   Ja! [Yes!]

YOUNG JABU   Wena? [With you?]

MADIBA   Ja! [Yeah!]

YOUNG JABU   Awuyona i type yami. [You are not my type.]

(*Silence – as the 'tsotsis' look at one another with incredulity. No one speaks to them this way. JABU has naively not understood the danger she is in.*)

MADIBA   (*With danger.*) Uthini? [What?] What did you
              just say to me?

YOUNG JABU   (*A little less certain.*) I said you are not my
              type!

              (*They start to laugh. Suddenly they grab her, spread her arms
              and take turns violently kicking, punching and beating her.
              They throw her to the ground. MADIBA grabs her by her T-
              shirt and pulls her up to within inches of his face.*)

MADIBA   (*Smiling viciously, he whispers.*) I am coming
              back for you! Sifebe! [Bitch!]

JABU (*Slowly getting to her feet.*) I couldn't tell Pappie. I couldn't tell
anyone. This was about the 'Ninjas': one of the most feared
gangs in Zola. So I kept silent and hoped the problem would
go away. But nothing just goes away!

              The gangsters surround her.

MADIBA   Woza! [Come!] (*Exploding.*) WOZA LA! [COME
              HERE!]

              (*She turns, and slowly moves towards him. She is terrified.
              MADIBA forces her onto the ground. She scrambles, trying to
              escape. The other 'tsotsis' grab her by the legs – dragging her
              back to Madiba, and delivering her at his feet. He smiles
              and takes out a gun. She starts to cry in terror. He points
              the barrel between her eyes, and then slowly runs the gun
              sensuously over her body. He lingers over her breasts and
              back towards her mouth.*)

              (*Whispering suggestively.*)
              Vula! [Open!] Vul'umlomo! [Open your mouth!]

GANGTERS   (*Screaming in rage.*) Vula sifebe! [Open bitch!]

(She opens her mouth. He thrusts the gun into it, until she is choking on the barrel and weeping with fear.)

MADIBA   If I see you on these streets again – I WILL rape you!

(Simply.) And then I'm going to kill you!

(He leans over and spits onto her face.)

Sifebe! [Bitch]

TSOTSI 2   *(Kicking her feet as he leaves.)* BITCH!

(BULLY finds JABU crying.)

BULLY   Jabu… Jabu…yini?
[Jabu… Jabu… what is it?]

(He holds her as she cries.)

YOUNG JABU   Bully! Ama Ninja azongenza noma yini…
[Bully, Bully! The Ninjas are going to do things to me…]
Angangibulala, angangi-raper!
[They're going to kill me… rape me!]
Mina ngiyahamba la e Zola!
[I have to leave Zola!]

JABU   I had no choice but to leave Zola.

(The family gather to say a hurried goodbye to JABU.)

PAPPIE   Hamba grand! Mntana wasedladleni.
[Go well. Farewell my sister.]

YOUNG JABU   OK Pappie!

Ma, sengiyahamba.

[Grandmother, goodbye.]

(*She hugs her GRANDMOTHER. She moves to BULLY who is not looking at her. She pulls him to her and they hug.*)

I'll miss you boy.

(*He turns away, trying not to cry.*)

JABU I left Bully and my family behind – and started building a new life for myself in Chiawelo. I would call home often to stay in contact – but time moves. The years run through your fingers like sand. Before I knew it....

(*JABU and BULLY are on the phone.*)

YOUNG JABU (*Singing as he laughs.*) Happy Birthday Bully! Happy Birthday to you!

JABU My little cousin Bully was turning 16 years old!

YOUNG JABU Bully...

(*She sings the first line of the clapping song they once sang as children. He joins in.*)

Katsamaya ma... Iye mh hm!

[I walked with... i-yeah mh mh!]

Le bo nkgono ma... Iye mh mh!

[Old ladies... i-yeah mh – hm!]

Ba babedi ma... Iye mh hm!

[There were two of them... i-yeah mh hm!]

(*They laugh together at the memory.*)

YOUNG JABU I miss you boy.

YAEL FARBER & THE CAST

| BULLY | Nami, sisi. [Me too, sister.] |

| YOUNG JABU | I'll see you on Sunday. |

JABU   I was working by then. I wanted to spoil him with a new pair of shoes. I went to Eastgate shopping mall that Saturday. I withdrew 500 Rands. I remember that morning so vividly. I walked around for hours looking at shoes.

> (*The other cast members stand in a line, holding pairs of shoes as though displayed in shop windows. They spin and move rapidly across the stage as she walks, creating the illusion of endless shoes for purchase.*)

There were so many shoes there, but I didn't buy any for uBully. I don't know why.

I bought nothing that morning…

Except…a black hat for myself.

That Sunday evening at eight, Bully was standing in our yard – when a single stray bullet from a pump-action shotgun hit him in the head.

> (*A cast member stands and fires a gun. The sound is as authentic, loud and brutal. JABU screams and falls to her knees. BULLY spins from the impact of the bullet – as though in slowed motion. A white sheet is thrown up and billows down onto an upturned zinc bath. BULLY lies unconscious, as though on a hospital bed.*)

| PAPPIE | Jabu! It's uBully…in intensive care. |

JABU   In the early hours of that morning – Bully came to me in a dream.

> (*BULLY's ghostly figure appears – as at the start of the story – in a shaft of light. Slowly he twists the white T-shirt he*

wears, in continuous circles around his torso. He is trapped and cannot break free. His face is shadowed. The cast sing.)

---

uYingcwele Baba

[You are holy my Lord.]

uYingcqwele.

[You are holy]

(He begs JABU to help him. She refuses – knowing that once he undresses, he will leave her forever.)

BULLY   Jabu… Help me. Help me to undress.

Ngisize ungikhumule! [Help me to undress!]

Ngisize ungikhumule, Jabu! [Help me to undress, Jabu!]

(Getting more desperate.) Help me Jabu! Help me to undress… I have to go now. Help me Jabu. Please Jabu. Help me!

Jabuuuuuuuuu…

(She starts awake. BULLY sighs deeply, as life leaves his body.)

JABU At five-thirty in the morning – the hospital called.

(They wrap BULLY in the sheet he lies on, and carry him to the floor, centre-stage – where they stand around him, as though at an open coffin viewing.)

Amagugu a le lizwe*

[Our prized, worldly goods]

---

* Lyrics from a traditional South African spiritual hymn commonly sung at funerals

Ayosala emathuneni

[Will not go with us to the grave]

Sengiyo lala ngingedwa ethuneni lami

[I will lie alone in my grave.]

Sengiyo lala ngingedwa ethuneni lami

[I will lie alone in my grave.]

JABU   The black hat I bought in Eastgate – I wore to his funeral. And the R500 for his shoes, we used for his burial.

> (*They cover BULLY with the blanket they played on as children. JABU and PAPPIE hug as they cry at the graveside.*)

Three years later, my Uncle Pappie was stabbed to death in Zola.

> (*PAPPIE looks back at JABU for the last time, smiles, and falls gently to the ground. GRANNY covers him with a blanket.*)

They say someone stabbed him for a can of beer.

> (*JABU sits between the two covered bodies.*)

I was filled with hatred. I hated Zola. I hated Soweto. I hated this country that lets 16 year olds die in their backyards on a Sunday night. I hated this place where we go to more funerals than weddings in our lives.

Out of that strong family I had in Zola – my Grandmother is alone there now. They say the young should bury the old. But in Soweto, Mzantsi Afrika… [South Africa…] The old bury the young.

> (*JABU takes the lead in the funeral song. The cast rise from their positions on the stage and remove the blankets, berets etc. they have worn for this story. They sing this funeral song with arms raised and eyes closed in exultation. It is a collective moment of grief – expressing the depth of a*

community's pain. JABU stands centre – as the others circle her singing.)

Amagugu a le lizwe

[Our prized, worldly goods]

Ayosala emathuneni

[Will not go with us to the grave]

Sengiyo lala ngingedwa ethuneni lami

[I will lie alone in my grave.]

Sengiyo lala ngingedwa ethuneni lami

[I will lie alone in my grave.]

(*They disappear into the shadows as TSHALLO takes centre stage.*)

(*TSHALLO stands in a shaft of light, as though in a doorway at night.*)

TSHALLO When I was a child, I was afraid of the dark. I hated putting the rubbish out at night. My uncle used to ask me: 'What is it out there that you are afraid of? You must find out so that you can fight it!' One night he locked me out in the dark…

> (*TSHALLO knocks frantically at the door, created with a zinc bath held vertically.*)

> YOUNG TSHALLO (*Pleading and terrified.*) Malume? Malume [Uncle] please! Vula! [Open!] Malume? [Uncle?] PLEASE!

TSHALLO I screamed for hours, until I had no fear left inside me. That night I understood that darkness…is nothing.

> (*He sings.*)

Dikopo tsa rona morena, O dimamele,

[Please Lord, listen to our requests]

O diutlwelle,

[Hear them,]

Oho morena

[Oh Lord]

(*Breaking into a smile.*) I grew up in Soshanguwe – Block K. It was a rough section of the township. Sello – my best friend and I – used to dream about ways to get out of there some day.

> (*They are young boys, talking passionately about football. TSHALLO has a pair of soccer boots, hanging by the laces, around his neck.*)

SELLO	Bona! Ke go botsa ka Amos Mkhari.
	[Listen! I am telling you about Amos Mkhari. (A famous South African football player from the '80s.)]

YOUNG TSHALLO	Wait! Nna ke go botsa ka Eric 'The Principal' Chippa Chauke.
	[I'm telling you about Eric Cheepa Chauke. (Another famous South African footballer of that decade.)]

(*He does some fancy footwork – imitating the style of his hero.*)

TSHALLO	Soccer was our only chance – our one-way ticket out of there. We ate, breathed and lived soccer.

(*Another boy joins them with an old radio. They gather around it, listening intensely to the commentary of a football game – spoken at great speed.*)

COMMENTATOR	Patson 'kamuzu' Banda – Oa e tsea Patson, o efa The Principal Chippa Chauke, The Principal o e sa mo gare ga lepatlego Jomo Sono – Jomo ore ke a feta, Howard Freeze oa e tsea o efa Ace Ntsoelengoe – The Principal o a mo tseela o e busetsa go Jomo Sono – Jomo Sono o efa Shakes Mashaba – Shakes o e busetsa go Jomo – Jomo o a tsena – o lebadi 18 area, otsena ka di 18 area, o a thala, o tsosa hlogo o a raga KA GA RE... 1 ORLANDO PIRATES, 0 KAIZER CHIEFS
	[Patson Kamuzu Banda – Patson throws it to The Principal Chippa Chauke, The Principal sends it over to the middle of the park to Jomo Sono, Jomo tries to get through but Howard Freeze intercepts and sends it to Ace Ntsolengoe but the Principal dispossess him and sends it back to Jomo, Jomo passes it on to Shakes Mashaba, Shakes sends

YAEL FARBER & THE CAST

it back to Jomo, Jomo is approaching the 18 area, he's in the 18 area, he dribbles past them, he raises his head, he kicks it, IT'S A GOAL! One Orlando Pirates, Nil Kaizer Chiefs!]

(All explode with joy as Jomo Sono scores a goal – hugging one another and screaming ecstatically.)

TSHALLO   The way they praised them – you would wish you could be them! We wanted that! We wanted to share the world of the Jomo Sonos! [Most celebrated football player of the '80s in South Africa]

Every Saturday morning, we were on the field practising.

(With intricate footwork and spectacular headers, they mime passing the ball back and forth between them. This sequence ends with a flourish, as THALLO imitates the famous Pele trademark goal technique. They applaud one another joyously.)

YOUNG TSHALLO   I'm telling you – some day I'll be wearing Black and White – playing for Orlando Pirates! [One of the most popular football teams in South Africa]

SELLO   I'll be in Gold and Black for Lekhosi! [Chiefs!] [Kaizer Chiefs is the other most successful South African football team, and respected rival of Orlando Pirates] Hola bakajuju! [Up the Buccaneers!]

YOUNG TSHALLO   Hola Lekhosi! [Up the Chiefs!]

TSHALLO   But Sello started to miss practice.

SELLO   Ah man, Tshallo! Ke busy. [I'm busy.]

YOUNG TSHALLO   *(Annoyed.)* O busy ka eng? [Busy with what?]

SELLO	Ko youth club. [At the youth club.]

YOUNG TSHALLO	(*Exasperated.*) Youth Club? What about our dream of playing professional soccer?

SELLO	Daar a Youth Club [There at the Youth Club…] Go na le dance, le drama gapegape go na le dicherrie. [There's dancing, drama and…there are girls there!]

TSHALLO	He said one magic word: women! I dumped my boots and followed him.

(*He arrives at the meeting. The song is dynamic and vibrant. Everyone is dancing in the style typical of the township youth movements during the 80s. The atmosphere is electric. The youth club members sing with pride and supreme confidence.*)

MEMBERS	Now! Is the time!* To change your mind! And build this nation! Mo Kiro…

(*Walking between the dancers – TSHALLO watches them wide-eyed.*)

TSHALLO	The meeting was held in a garage. This was the most vibrant atmosphere I had ever been in. And the women!!! Babengishaya ngaphakathi. [Drove me wild!]

(*The women move centre and begin to move to the growing intensity of the drum beat. TSHALLO moves centre and proudly dances 'Indlamu', a form of traditional Zulu dance.*

* An anthem sung at the KIRO Youth Club – a movement created by the Roman Catholic Church in South Africa, dedicated to politically conscientising the black youths in the townships.

(The women ululate wildly. The dance ends as T... falls back onto the floor and the others applaud. ... group together – suddenly quiet and intense, staring at the audience.)

Behind a door in that garage, secret meetings were being held. I started to understand: Kiro was no dance and drama club. They were mobilising the youth! We were young and black… And our time had come.

(The company begins the pulse of a growing toyi-toyi – the famous form of protest unique to the uprising of the liberation movement in South Africa. The cast pulsate with energy and power.)

I wanted to be involved – and then suddenly – I was in!

'Azikhwelwa'; ['Stay Aways';] Operation 'Clean-up'; Night vigils. It was the year of 'Black Christmas'.

(The sound of the toyi-toyi swells and then falls.)

I was 15 years old and *shit-scared*, but I was in too deep to walk away now. And when you are in – you are in. There is no turning back!

(The toyi-toyi grows to its climax as the cast closes in on the audience.)

Kom Guerillas – Masoja!*

[Come guerrillas – soldiers!]

Kom Guerillas – Masoja!

[Come guerrillas – soldiers!]

Nelson Mandela – Ubaba Wethu!

[Nelson Mandela – our father!]

* Commonly chanted lyrics which accompanied the toyi-toyi during South Africa's years of the Political Resistance struggle. Toyi-Toyi is a dynamic melange of marching, foot stamping and rhythmic chanting, and has come to symbolise the crowd's expression of anger during the Apartheid years.

Oliver Thambo – Isoja!

[Oliver Thambo – a soldier!]

Kuthi Ngihlanye! Masoja!

[I want to lose my mind! Soldiers!]

> (*They scatter and gather upstage, holding a white sheet aloft by it corners, creating a canopy over* TSHALLO.)

TSHALLO It's raining. I'm in a tent. It smells of sweat and anger in here. We were afraid of nothing…except Pretoria North Riot Squad.

They were so brutal. They fired tear gas into the tent.

> (*The tent collapses and writhes with bodies beneath it. Everyone is tangled in the sheet and each other – desperately trying to breathe.*)

I can't see. I can't breathe. I feel like I'm dying.

> (*They run from the tent, gasping for breath, and splash water on their faces from the enamel bowls on the stage periphery. They all climb into a zinc bath – huddled together, whispering and crying – afraid of being discovered by the brutal Riot Squad.*)

We find someone's coal box to hide in. I'm not alone. There are others hiding in here with me. Some are crying in pain. Others have fainted.

SSSSSHH!

> (*The others fall silent.*)

Silence…

YOUNG TSHALLO (*At the end of his tether.*) Ama comrades…I am going home.

ALL No Tshallo! They'll see you!

(*They try and convince him not to leave, as it will reveal their hiding place. TSHALLO however will not be deterred. He steps out of the 'coal box' but stops dead in his tracks.*)

YOUNG TSHALLO Fuck! They've seen me!

(*They all scatter, screaming. TSHALLO grabs a passing woman in the panic and chaos.*)

Sista, mpontshe tsela ya go ya gae please!
[Sister, help me find my way home please!]
Please! Show me the safest way home.

(*She shakes him off and runs into the dark.*)

TSHALLO Alone in the dark, stinking of petrol – not knowing my way home… Police everywhere…I didn't stand a chance. But then suddenly Sello was beside me. He came back for me.

(*They crouch in the shadows – waiting for the police vehicles to pass.*)

SELLO (*Quickly explaining the quickest route home.*)
Tshallo! Kamo go tletse maphodisa I mora
[Don't take this road because the police are all over. Take that road]
and just over the fence, Jo – you are home.

(*They split off in different directions – but TSHALLO stops and calls to SELLO in the dark.*)

YOUNG TSHALLO Sello…

(*SELLO turns back to look at TSHALLO.*)

Ta Bru! [Thank you brother!]

SELLO (*Whispering.*) Don't forget Tshallo – some day all this shit will be over…and you…

You gonna be the next Jomo Sono!

(*They smile at one another for a moment.*)

Hola Bakajuju! [Up the Buccaneers!]

YOUNG TSHALLO Hola Lekhosi! [Up the Chiefs!]

(*SELLO disappears into the dark.*)

TSHALLO I made it home safely that night. But Sello didn't.

The Police took him and several other young boys behind a hill…

(*The other cast members group together on the upturned bath with their backs to the audience.*)

And hanged them all!

(*Their right arms shoot up to portray the ropes. They sway slowly in unison as hanging corpses.*)

I don't know how long they were there… But when we found them… They were rotten!

(*The raised arms turn into the black power salute of raised fists. They turn to face the audience and fan out – their eyes haunted and filled with rage. They sing.*)

Phambili! Phambili siyaya!*

[Forward! Forward we go!]

Siyaya nomakubi!

[We go forward – even if it is bad!]

Noma besidubula!

[Even if they shoot us with their guns!]

* A protest song of the Resistance movement in South Africa, sung by the masses during marches and confrontations with Riot Squads attempting to break up mass protests. Also sung at funerals of fallen political activists.

YAEL FARBER & THE CAST

Besishaya!

[Beating us with their batons!]

Besibulala!

[Even if they kill us!]

Siyaya – nomakubi!

[We go forward – even when it's bad!]

Phambili siyaya!

[Forward we go.]

Siphuma esoviet, sipheth' amabhazuka.

[We come from the Soviet, with our AK 47s.]

Siyaya nomakubi!

[Forward we go!]

TSHALLO And so I would get up day after day – week after week – and do what I did yesterday, or last week. What I knew I would do tomorrow. I ran. I hid. We buried our dead.

> (*As* TSHALLO *and company sing at the funeral of fallen friends, a cast member moves upstage to the tin bath and begins to shovel the sand contained in the bath across the stage. The sand is dry – and the air is soon thick with dust, which rises like a smog from the stage. The image of a township funeral is brought vividly to life, as the audience and cast share the pervading smell and texture of the dirt.*)

Funeral after funeral...

I got to a point where it became nothing.

If I died – if they died – it didn't matter. They could do whatever they wanted – but forward...forward we go!

> (*They advance on the audience in the swirling dust, eyes filled with anger and grief – portraying the countless adolescents – TSHALLO amongst them – who faced down war vehicles with nothing but stones in their hands.*)

Phambili siyaya!

[Forward we go.]

Siphuma esoviet, sipheth' amabhazuka.

[We come from the Soviet, with our AK 47s.]

Siyaya nomakubi!

[Forward we go!]

(*They all are on their haunches in the sand singing, taking a break from the relentless running and violence.*)

TSHALLO I don't know what other people were doing at 15 years old – but we were trying to survive. Doing the best we could – just to stay alive.

We kept our ears open for word on the street.

(*They all look up suddenly in fear.*)

Kwanyiwa! [We're going to shit!] It's bad today. Just down the road there is a car taking people. They've come for boys on our block.

(*The sound of Pretoria North Riot squad is created vocally by the cast. It is an ominous pulsating sound of multiple sirens throbbing in the air – as portrayed in TIPO's story.*)

YOUNG TSHALLO (*Panicking.*) I can't sleep at home tonight.
This time it could be me.
Make a plan.
Make a plan.
Make a plan.

TSHALLO Everyone made a plan. But some sold out!

(*They turn on a man who has betrayed them by informing on political activists to the Security Police.*)

YOUNG TSHALLO Mayishisw'impimpi! [Burn the spy / informer!]

YAEL FARBER & THE CAST

OTHERS   Mayishisw'impimpi! [Burn the spy / informer!]

(They roll a giant tyre to the centre of the stage. They force the informer into the tyre – and pulling his T-shirt off him, throw a match into the tyre, which bursts into flames. This creates the illusion of burning the accused man alive. He screams frantically, as TSHALLO covers his ears to block out the reality of what he has witnessed. He sings as the screams fade away.)

Dikopo tsa rona morena, O dimamele,

[Please Lord, listen to our requests]

O diutlwelle,

[Hear them,]

Oho morena

[Oh Lord]

(The cast are gathered around the smouldering tyre. TSHALLO moves forward to address the audience.)

TSHALLO   I know we've heard these stories before. 'Let's move on!' we say. But we don't know how to – because we haven't really looked back yet. We all went our separate ways and left those years behind us. But those years shaped us. We were children. This story is not about 'umzabalazo' [the Struggle] – it's about me… and most of us who grew up in the townships.

I don't want your pity. I just want to remember who I was before all of this…who I could've been without all the dust and the blood and the pain of living in that darkness. I just want to remember that little boy who cried because once, he was afraid of the dark. I don't remember what it is to be afraid anymore…

And sometimes… I wish I could.

(They all circle the smouldering tyre and begin to sing the call and refrain with which they began the show. They each stand, as at the start of the play, in single white beams of light. The singing continues as each cast member addresses the audience in turn.)

BONGI All my life – I waited for the past to pass… A country I would never have to visit again. But I have stood between the mountains on the river's edge. And I know: for better or worse – that small village was my home. I would not have been given my suffering if I did not have the strength to survive. With this knowledge I face the future. I pray. I give thanks. I rise.

> (*The song swells, as* BONGI *raises her arms, closes her eyes and sings with emotion and exultation.*)

ROELF We cannot leave things in the dust without a decent burial. No matter how small.

TIPO We all have to stand in the rain and wash away the pain.

> (*They all raise their arms, as though being cleansed by the rain.*)

JABU Like a huge grave we have to dig and reclaim what was once forgotten or cast aside.

> (*They all drop to their knees in the dust, and gather handfuls of sand, chanting.*)

BONGI Uthuli Eluthulini. [Ashes to ashes, dust to dust.]

JABU Umlotha Emlotheni. [Ashes to ashes, dust to dust.]

TSHALLO Mmu Mmung. [Ashes to ashes, dust to dust.]

TIPO Molora Moroleng. [Ashes to ashes, dust to dust.]

ROELF Ashes to ashes and dust to dust.

(They stand with their hands cupped in front of them – holding handfuls of dust.)

TSHALLO And from the dust – Like doves...we will rise.

(They lift and open their arms, walking toward the audience, with dust pouring through their fingers. They sing.)

Thina, thina sinjengamajuba*
[We are like doves]
Thina, thina sinjengamajuba
[We are like doves]
Thina, thina sinjengamajuba
[We are like doves]

(A zinc bath is placed centre – and they pour the water from their original enamel bowls into the collective zinc bath. Each cast member kneels in turn and washes – cleansing themselves of the past as the others sing fragments from the songs of their stories. The washing is joyous for some – tender for others. JABU throws a shower of water over her head, laughing as the others sing:)

Thina, thina sinjengamajuba
[We are like doves]
Thina, thina sinjengamajuba
[We are like doves]

(ROELF bends over the bath, smiling, and splashes himself with water as the others sing:)

Die son het gaan saak onder by die wingerd. Ons is baie honger
[The sun has set, it's under the vineyard. We are very hungry.]

* Lyrics from a traditional South African spiritual hymn commonly sung in church & community contexts.

YAEL FARBER & THE CAST

Die son het gaan saak onder by die wingerd. Ons is b
honger

[The sunhas set it's under the vineyard. We are very hungry.]

Gee ons die 'jive' – Ons wil nou huis toe gaan.

[Give us the jive. We want to go home now]

Gee ons die 'jive' – Ons wil nou huis toe gaan.

[Give us the jive. We want to go home now.]

(*TSHALLO then kneels reverentially at the bath. Filling his cupped hands with water, he washes himself, as he and the cast sing:*)

Dikopo tsa rona morena, O dimamele,

[Please Lord, listen to our requests]

O diutlwelle,

[Hear them,]

Oho morena

[Oh Lord]

(*As TSHALLO's singing concludes, TIPO suddenly lunges towards an exit, attempting to run away. The others catch him in time, and smiling – they point to the bath. TIPO resigns himself to his fate. He winks at the audience, and jumps without hesitation into the bath. He splashes wildly, anointing himself, as the others dance around the bath, showered by the water he is throwing over himself. The cast and TIPO sing:*)

Njalo, njalo, njalo

[Always, always, always]

Siya thandaza, siyanikela

[We pray, we offer]

Siya dumisa, njalo

[We praise Him, always]

(*Finally,* BONGI *steps into the bath – arms outstretched. Supported by the others, she is lowered into the water. She closes her eyes, smiling, and sings:*)

O Lerato – O Lerato – O Lerato

[You are Love – You are Love – You are Love]

Morena Jesu.

[Lord Jesus.]

(*They cast gather together behind the bath. Raising their arms slowly – as though releasing a flock of doves, spent in energy – yet exuding a resilience and joy, they gaze out towards the future and sing:*)

Thina, thina sinjengamajuba

[We are like doves]

Thina, thina sinjengamajuba

[We are like doves]

Thina, thina sinjengamajuba

[We are like doves]

(*Blackout.*)

HE LEFT QUIETLY

Conceived & written by Yael Farber

A HISTORY OF TEXT AND PRODUCTION DEVELOPMENT

In 1984, Duma Kumalo was sentenced to death by hanging for his alleged participation in the mob killing of a town councillor in Sharpeville, South Africa. The trial was a miscarriage of justice that was hardly exceptional in Apartheid South Africa. The case of the Sharpeville Six (as Kumalo and his co-accused became known) did, however, capture the attention of the world – and bring to light the extent to which the South African justice system was deeply corrupt. 15 hours before they were due to be hanged – under intense international pressure – the state granted them a stay of execution. Kumalo served a further four years of a life sentence in prison. After seven years' incarceration for a crime he did not commit, he was released as part of political negotiations.

Yael Farber first met Duma Kumalo after seeing him in the production, *The Story I Am About to Tell*, in Grahamstown in 2001. Farber approached Kumalo, asking how she might be involved in his story being told. Their original intention was to write a book about his experiences on Death Row. The two met over several months, at times going away to work in isolation outside of Johannesburg. During this time Farber conducted a series of intensive interviews with Kumalo, collating the material intended for his biography. However, when Farber was approached by the In Transit festival in Berlin, Germany at the Haus der Kultur to create a new theatre production, she proposed Duma Kumalo's story as the subject matter. It was over the course of the next five weeks that the theatre production *He Left Quietly* was born. Farber had, by this stage, created *A Woman in Waiting* and *Amajuba* in the years previously. More experienced in the creation of testimonial theatre, she decided to experiment with the genre. The enormity of Kumalo's life experience and the impact that Kumalo had as a presence on the lives of those who encountered him, inspired Farber to work in a different way from the two previous works.

She cast an actor to portray a young version of Duma Kumalo – affording Kumalo the dignity and stillness of sitting and telling his story, without the freneticism required of both narrating and enacting. Ten days prior to the

Berlin premier of the work, Farber approached her assistant director and stage manager Yana Sakelaris to join the cast, portraying a character which Farber decided was necessary in order to reach out to portray the white community's relationship to injustice, indifference and accountability. This new development in the shaping of the text and production put Farber and her cast under considerable stress so close to the Berlin premiere. The show opened to positive response – though Farber understood this to be the start of a journey towards exploring the most potent way of telling Kumalo's story for the stage. The production returned to Africa – where Farber further developed the material for its South African premiere at The National Arts Festival in Grahamstown. The production was received with acclaim from audiences and critics alike. Tours to Europe followed to great success – with a season at The State Theatre in Pretoria, upon their return to South Africa. The last live presentation of the work was to an audience of legal judges and prosecutors – some of whom had been practising in a system that had once sentenced Kumalo to death. It was Farber and Kumalo's intention to continue presenting the production.

Duma Joshua Kumalo, however, died an untimely death at the age of 49 in 2006.

The case was never reopened – and to this day, Kumalo's name has never been cleared.

DIRECTOR'S PROGRAMME NOTE

It is impossible to come away from any single conversation with Duma Joshua Kumalo without having learned something new about yourself or the world. He has faced death and passionately chooses to face life – despite experiencing the ultimate cruelties people are capable of inflicting upon one another. He never shies away from describing, in great detail, the darkest memories that constitute his experiences. But always there emanates from him a sense of man's worth; a dignity and humanity that has survived against unimaginable odds. Duma has a way of sharing his story that extends far beyond himself. He reaches out in ways that impact profoundly on anyone who meets him. I have attempted to articulate the impact he has on others – by representing a story within his story. It is these connections that root us to our common humanity. Lives collide in ways that we can never anticipate. *He Left Quietly* seeks to challenge our notions of time and space – in the act of tangibly facing the past and being accountable when called upon to contribute to the process of healing. *He Left Quietly* is an examination of what can happen if you open yourself to other people's stories – and allow the retelling of histories to bring a sense of value to your own. Duma has a gentle manner that belies his immensely harsh suffering. There is an almost incomprehensible lack of judgement and hatred in his recounting of the past. But make no mistake! This is a man who is driven by a powerful will to have his story told and heard. In whatever way he can tell it – to anyone who will listen. *He Left Quietly* is not the first telling of his experiences – nor, I am certain, will it be the last. It is simply a great privilege to be one of those who had the opportunity to engage with this exceptional story and the man who somehow survived it – with his sense of humour, his faith in humanity and his compassion inexplicably intact.

Yael Farber
Berlin, Germany, Premier Performance, 2003

HE LEFT QUIETLY

Created with and based on the life of Duma Kumalo

This work is performed ideally in a 'space' rather than a formalized theatre, and on the floor to a raked audience – as opposed to on a raised stage – so that contact with the audience is immediate and dynamic. The integrity of the production depends upon the audience experiencing themselves as active participants rather than passive voyeurs.

A chair stands centre stage. On the floor are three steel mesh cages laid flat. In this configuration, they are unnoticed or create a floor that appears as a grid. Once raised, they are opened like 'book flats' – creating free-standing 'walls' of caging. These will be manipulated and used in various ways throughout the story to represent the prison environment.

Up stage left of the chair is a pile of old green uniforms, behind which are two free standing white enamel toilets. Up-stage right of the chair is a mound of old shoes (about 50 pairs). Both the uniforms and shoes are 'found objects' – the actual items we retrieved from South Africa's Death Row, and worn by its condemned before the death penalty was finally banished in South Africa. It is likely that within the pile of uniforms and shoes, were those once worn by DUMA KUMALO and his co-accused.

Beneath the pile of Green Death Row uniforms – unbeknown to the audience – an actor (who will portray the YOUNG DUMA) lies hidden. He will enact DUMA's memories as they are recalled. But for the audience's entrance into the performance space, and until YOUNG DUMA stirs and emerges from the pile, the audience remain completely unaware of his presence.

Amongst the audience sits a WOMAN in her mid-thirties. She is white and nondescript.

She has a note pad and pen on her lap, and cigarettes in her pocket. She is indistinguishable from the other audience members. Her status as a member of the production's cast will only be revealed when she begins to speak.

or opens in the venue – if possible allowing a flood of light onto the performance area: a moment's contact with the world outside this performance. Enter DUMA KUMALO – a striking, tall man in his mid-forties – though his age is indistinguishable. The years of suffering have created a mien of age beyond his years. His face is weather-beaten. His teeth fan outwards from years of grinding as a result of nightmares. He is dressed in a denim shirt and jeans – but apparent beneath his shirt is the dark green uniform of South Africa's former Death Row. He carries a quaint suitcase made of cardboard and found objects. This is the authentic case DUMA – like other prisoners – constructed in jail, while serving his Life Sentence. It is filled with handwritten letters.

He walks slowly and without affectation towards the chair, takes a cigarette from his pocket, lights it and sits. He looks up at the audience. The audience looks back. A silence ensues. This is not a hostile silence. DUMA emanates calm – though his presence has an unnerving intensity. He will smoke incessantly throughout the piece – as he did during his years of incarceration. At the peak of the tension created by the silence, he exhales a cloud of smoke, nods and quietly begins.)

DUMA When does the soul leave the body?… At which precise moment?
Does it leave with our last breath?… Or the final beat of our heart?
Is it possible that I stayed here amongst you – the living – long after my soul quietly left my body behind?
In my life I have died many times. But here I am again and again – alive.
I am Duma Joshua Kumalo. Prisoner Number V 34-58. In 1984 I was condemned to death for a crime I did not commit.
I spent three years on Death Row, and a further four years of a Life Sentence. I have been measured for the length of my coffin; the size of the rope for my neck;

I took my last sacrament; I said – to my broken father – a final goodbye. (*Smiling gently.*) And with each of these moments, my soul left my body behind. The dead leave the living with a burden. When going to their deaths – they would shout to us: Those who survive – tell the world!

(*Pause as he looks at the audience.*)

I speak for them.
They live in me.
Perhaps it is they who are talking when I open my mouth.
I cannot undo the past.
I cannot change what happened to me.
And so I live with what I have seen – on borrowed time.

(*In a chanting style, reciting his traditional praise names:*)

Duma hamba uyoDuma ezizweni – uNoDumo uhleli kaMenzi. [Go Duma and be famous worldwide…]

(*This is the start of DUMA's traditional Zulu Praise Names. Pauses as he smokes and nods.*)

Life is mystery.
The road turns in ways we could never imagine. I took the wrong road one morning… And never came back the same man.
Who would I have been if I had not taken that road? Impossible to say…
Because from inside Death Row – you find your own voice before you die. You see your own truth.
You finally understand the meaning of your own name.
Duma Joshua Kumalo.
V 34-589.

(A woman sitting inconspicuously in the audience lights a cigarette. Lights grow on her. She speaks quietly, without affectation or presentation.)

WOMAN 'Remember the past. Live the present. Trust the future. But never forget.'

I grew up on those words. The legacy of pain we inherit:

The Truth of our Fathers. But every country we run to has its own history. And the pain of where we come from goes with us to new lands. We bow our heads, thankful it is not us this time.

But if we have our father's eyes... What have we seen? And how did we forget?

DUMA Case Number 861 of the Truth and Reconciliation Commission for Human Rights Violations.

WOMAN Sebokeng. August 5th 1996. He testified.

DUMA Duma Joshua Kumalo, V3458.

WOMAN What do we do? I asked him afterwards on the dust road outside the hall. Go home and forget?

DUMA Help me write what I remember – help me speak for the dead.

WOMAN I am here to observe...

DUMA Where is home – if you are just here to watch? What country are you running to – if you are just a bystander here? ... A guest...

WOMAN   I'm not running…

DUMA   You are in or you are out.

(The WOMAN rises from her seat in the audience and moves into the performance space.)

WOMAN   We agreed to meet the following week.

(The lights shift. DUMA is alone on the chair. Smoke from his cigarette gathers in the light shaft over him. His face is shadowed.)

DUMA   Amanzi angihaqa kwaza kwaba nasekuphileni kwami.*
[The waters closed in over me.]
Utwa lwangikaka.
[The deep engulfed me.]
Umhlanga wathandela ekhanda lami.
[Reeds were wrapped around my head.]
Ngehla ngasemikhawulweni yezintaba.
[I sank to the base of the mountain.]
Imigoqo yomhlaba yayisemva kwami kuze kube phakade.
[I went down to the land whose bars closed over me forever.]

(During the above incantation – from beneath the pile of prison uniform, as though a memory has been stirred – a young version of DUMA slowly rises. He peels the old green uniforms away that are covering him. Emanating intensity, he stands, and walks in a protracted, extended manner. The walk serves to heighten the visual, non-literal nature of memory. He circles DUMA and moves to lean against the back wall, where he lights a cigarette.)

* Jonah, 2: 6–7

1

DUMA Monday morning began like any other day.

Sharpeville South Africa 1984.

People who could hardly afford to feed their children were protesting another raise in the rents. I was never a political animal. Much happier to smoke Craven A, drink Castle Lager, spend time at the shebeen [pub] and think of Mandozi my girlfriend. But when people are marching in Sharpeville 1984 – you don't ask questions. You go!

As I stepped out onto Zwane Street that morning and joined the protest.

(*The YOUNG DUMA steps away from the wall and onto the 'road' before him. He breathes deeply, slowly and audibly.*)

I had no idea where that road would lead me.

And that in many ways – I would never again come home.

(*The WOMAN crosses behind the YOUNG DUMA and watches him walk his path.*)

Police opened fire with rubber bullets. A man next to me was shot in the ankle.

(*YOUNG DUMA moves between rubber bullets. With fluid movement, he lifts and places the WOMAN across his broad shoulders, and carries her to safety.*)

I carried him to his house and washed the wound. Then I went home. Later I heard the mob regrouped and marched to Town Councilor Jacob Dlamini's house. He was shot dead and burnt on the bonnet of his car.

WOMAN	Who killed that man?

DUMA	There were many people there. I cannot speak for them – Only for me. And when Jacob Dlamini died – I was not there.

WOMAN	They came for you three months later at four in the morning.

(*Speaking in Afrikaans – the* WOMAN *offers the voices of 'white authority' throughout the piece:*)

Wie is Duma?
[Who is Duma?]

(*Both* DUMA *and* YOUNG DUMA *look up.*)

BOTH DUMAS	I am.

WOMAN	Get dressed and bring your id! [Identity Document]

DUMA	I had no idea why. Outside dawn had not broken. Police cars and lights everywhere... I went quietly into the dark morning...

Into the waiting car.

(*The* YOUNG DUMA *raises his hands and moves slowly along the back wall and into a waiting police car. The song 'Rozi my Girl' plays unobtrusively. The sound crackles from an old LP.*)

WOMAN	(*Reading from a book.*) 'Internationally known as the Sharpeville Six, Duma Kumalo and his co-accused were convicted for the murder of Jacob Dlamini on the grounds of Common Purpose. A legal doctrine establishing guilt through causality and effect – in Apartheid South Africa this meant that simply being

in the vicinity of a murder was sufficient evidence to condemn a man to death.'

DUMA Hey Mandozi, my sweet 'cherrie' [colloquial term for 'girl'].

I remember the first time I saw you – in your school uniform on your way to school. That shy smile... You were my 'mshoza'... 'ntombi'... 'ithekeni', 'itsheri' from the day we met. [colloquial terms for girlfriend]

Ja! Yes! Mandozi! You were the one for me.

(*The song 'Rozi my Girl' ends.*)

WOMAN (*The voice of the writer asking questions – but suggesting the role of the interrogating officer.*)

Wat het op die 3de September gebeur?
[What happened on the 3rd of September?]

YOUNG DUMA (*Exhausted from the interrogation.*)

After the police opened fire – I left the scene. I went home.

WOMAN Jy's 'n slang Kaffir!*
[You are a snake Kaffir (derogatory term for a black person)]

Weet jy wat ons doen met slange?
[Do you know what we do with snakes?]

We shoot them in the head!

DUMA (*Wistful, lost in memory.*) Mandozi, Mandozi! You were the only one for me.

* Duma Kumalo's recall of Warrant Officer Schoeman's words to him during his interrogation.

YAEL FARBER & DUMA KUMALO

2

WOMAN   You are detained for five months before the case goes to trial. Under Section 29 – you have no rights to see a lawyer, a doctor or your family. But being a Christian State – we give you a Bible.

YOUNG DUMA   (*Pacing with a grey prison blanket around his shoulders, smoking and reading the Book of Job from the prison-issued Bible.*) 'Because our days upon earth are a shadow Behold God will not cast away an innocent man, Nor will he uphold the evil-doers.'*

DUMA   That was the hottest summer on the Highveld [a plateau area of South Africa containing eastern Gauteng and southern Mpumalanga] that anyone could remember. Endless days followed by wild rain falls.

WOMAN   As children we would run bare feet along the lilaque carpets of jacaranda blossoms in the white suburban streets after those tropical summer storms.

DUMA   Time passes in ways you cannot imagine. Five months of solitude waiting for the trial.

YOUNG DUMA   'Thou hast fashioned me as clay, And wilt thou bring me into dust again? Thou hast clothed me with skin and flesh And knit me together with bones and sinews.' †

* Job, 8: 9
† Job, 10: 9

DUMA   Five months of nothing but me and that Bible; the heat and the minutes that take hours – and hours that are minutes and months that suddenly slip away.

YOUNG DUMA   'Are not my days few?
Cease then and let me alone,
that I may take comfort a little.
Before I go whence I shall not return.'*

DUMA   It was during those months of detention, I tried to take my own life.

(*He drops a glass. The YOUNG DUMA picks up the shards and begins to eat them.*)

WOMAN   Broken glass from a window pane. You shit blood in the toilet…

(*YOUNG DUMA squats and cries out. A pool of blood grows beneath him.*)

They take you to the doctor. But within hours you are back in your cell.

(*YOUNG DUMA is sitting with his back to the audience rocking. He has a metal bucket in his hand. He strikes brutally at his leg and foot. The WOMAN turns away.*)

You try to break the bones in your legs…

DUMA   Just to see the outside world.

(*DUMA laughs.*)

There are four gaps in my mouth where good teeth were pulled during that time.

* Job, 10: 20

WOMAN   (*Looking into his open mouth.*) Healthy teeth extracted? Why?

DUMA   (*Laughing.*) A visit to the dentist meant that on the way there – if I looked out the car window – I could see the sky.

(*They look at each other for a long moment.*)

WOMAN   (*Standing, gathering her pages.*) What time tomorrow?

DUMA   (*Smiles, exhaling smoke.*) Time passes in ways you cannot imagine.

3

(*The WOMAN turns from DUMA, walks around him and stops behind his chair. DUMA continues to drag on his cigarette, lost in thought. She turns to the audience to address them directly.*)

WOMAN   What is the act of bearing witness?

A universal ritual in which one's pain is acknowledged.

Every story is silent until it has a listener. In 1996, the process began. The Truth and Reconciliation Commission's exhuming of memories…exhuming of graves: recovering remains of loved ones murdered by the State. Attendance at these hearings was predominantly black. The solitary white would arrive and sit to listen. But mostly – we didn't want to know. Some of us heard the testimonies broadcast on Sunday nights. Driving home and listening to the radio. Stop the car. Stop and listen!

Just stop!

Stunned – but not surprised.

You don't grow up in South Africa not knowing.

You know.

Where were we when the truth was finally being told?

How could there be empty chairs in those halls?

And if the truth falls on empty chairs – does it make a sound?

(*Miriam Makeba's voice filters through on an old LP. The YOUNG DUMA walks slowly across the stage and circles DUMA. He wears a brown jacket.*)

DUMA Four months before my arrest, I saw a pair of new shoes. They were in the window of John Craig in Vereeniging.

(*YOUNG DUMA stares into a shop window.*)

Buying shoes is an act of hope and confidence!

199 Rands! [South African currency]

'Church' shoes [colloquial expression for formal shoes] are not cheap…

The salesman told me they were life time guaranteed.

(*Laughing.*) Shit!

I didn't know I was buying shoes for my own trial
– and that I would never ever wear those shoes again.

WOMAN Stilte in die hof!
[Silence in the court!]

YAEL FARBER & DUMA KUMALO

Accused Number Seven – please rise. Before your sentencing – have you anything to say to this court?

YOUNG DUMA 'My lord, I laid my case before you. You heard much evidence that, according to me, was lies. Notwithstanding that, you have decided to accept that type of evidence against me. I have nothing further to say. Let the law take its course. That is all.'*

DUMA On Friday the 13th of December, after a three-month trial – though I had an alibi, and evidence that the only witness against me had lied, the judge passed sentence:

WOMAN Tell Accused Number Seven that the God of this world has no mercy on him.

He will be taken back to a place of custody – where he will hang by the neck until he is dead.

(*DUMA is singing a childhood song softly to himself.*)

DUMA

Sizinyoni thina Sizinyoni (*x 2*)†
[We are birds, we are birds]
Siyagxuma, Siyahlala
[We jump/fly and sit]
Sizinyoni
[We are birds.]

(*YOUNG DUMA moves backwards as though in a vortex. All that remains where he stood are his church shoes. He finds himself on the mound of Death Row uniforms.*)

* Duma Kumalo's actual words to the Judge, before sentence was passed.

† An old Zulu song, sung by children. Its origin is unknown.

My mother was a storyteller.

We would sit around the embowla [large tin barrel-drum in which a coal fire is built for warmth during winter on the streets and in poorer township homes] every night in the kitchen and listen to her stories. Neither fat nor thin. Neither tall nor short.

Thembekile Magdelene Hadebe Khumalo was a deeply religious woman. Like most township mothers…she was also a thief.

(*Laughing.*) She would steal bread, sugar, butter – anything for us – from the white family she cleaned for during the week. On Fridays, she would bring home the children's clothes to be washed. And for the weekend she would let us wear those clothes like they belonged to us. Come Monday morning they were back with their rightful owners in the suburbs – all traces of Sharpeville hand-washed out of them by my mother and her Sunlight Soap.

WOMAN   We had no idea.

DUMA   About what?

WOMAN   So many things… So many things.

4

(*The haunting sound of a multitude of men saying The Lord's Prayer rumbles through the space. Neon lights flicker on above. The cages are raised by DUMA and the WOMAN – forming a corridor, along which YOUNG DUMA moves into Death Row. YOUNG DUMA and DUMA exhale*

(simultaneously. DUMA *walks behind* YOUNG DUMA, *shadowing him.)*

YOUNG DUMA   Phefumula. Breathe.

DUMA   Try to remember to breathe.

YOUNG DUMA   Amanzi angihaqa kwaza kwaba nasekuphileni kwami.
[The waters closed in over me.]
Utwa lwangikaka.
[The deep engulfed me.]
Umhlanga wathandela ekhanda lami.
[Reeds were wrapped around my head.]
Ngehla ngasemikhawulweni yezintaba.
[I sank to the base of the mountain.]
Imigoqo yomhlaba yayisemva kwami kuze kube phakade.
[I went down to the land whose bars closed over me forever.]

DUMA   Death Row is the quietest place I have ever been. Like being buried at the bottom of a mountain. No one is permitted to talk… We are issued uniforms that are unwashed. They smell of the dead men who wore them until their final week. They find the shortest pants to give me – because I am tallest… And they give me two left shoes.

It is difficult to walk.

Don't worry – they tell me smiling. You don't have far to go.

Deep at the end of the corridor, I hear a group of men praying and crying. It's a sound I will never forget. This is the section where they put the men whose numbers have been called and will die in a week. It's called the 'Pot' – the guards explain – because that's where you will 'cook in your own fear'. In there, men can make as much noise as they want: A special privilege for those about to die.

The Guards wink at each other. For my first night on Death Row – they put me right next to this section. I try to sleep. I can hear the men preparing to die – singing, praying, screaming through the night.

For the first time since my mother died when I was a boy – I cry like a child.

(*YOUNG DUMA – hands over his ears – curls up in the grey blanket, as the sound of the condemned men fills the room. DUMA nods and smokes, as the light shaft over him dies.*

A morning bell rings. It is brutal and abrupt.)

WOMAN At six am a bell wakes you up each day.

(*The buzz continues.*)

At seven am you can shower if you want.

DUMA (*Shouting, as though down a corridor.*) Shower! Shower!

YOUNG DUMA You have taken everything, now you want me to wash?

(*In anguish.*) VOETSEK! FOK OFF! [Piss off! Fuck off!]

DUMA I refuse to clean myself. Quickly I start to look and smell of neglect. The guards have a special name for me: Mgodoyi! [Dog!] Dog!

WOMAN Eight am is breakfast.

You get soft porridge and cold coffee shoved in the door.

YAEL FARBER & DUMA KUMALO

Ten am is exercise in a hall. You must all walk in cir
in the same direction. If anyone is caught talking –
everyone is punished and sent back to their cells.

DUMA   Almal in! [Everyone in!] Almal in! [Everyone in!]

WOMAN   Eleven am is Lunch. And Supper – the last meal of the
day – is served at three o'clock.

DUMA   It's too early for supper – but the guards want to knock
off early.

WOMAN   Days on Death Row are endless but short.

DUMA   You have so much you want to say when you know you
are going to die. But you have to be silent – waiting for
four pm…when the bell finally rings.

*(A bell rings. The noise of men shouting, singing, arguing,
praying explodes in the auditorium. YOUNG DUMA gets his
mouth in front of the small opening in the cell caged door
– and shouts frantically down the corridor.)*

We talk, we sing, we shout to each other in our cells…

Because we know in four hours – silence must fall.

(The bell rings. There is an instant, eerie silence.)

Eight pm is bedtime – but on Death Row…

WOMAN   Suicide Watch…the lights never go out.

DUMA   Bulbs burn twenty-four hours in the cells.

WOMAN   There is no night or day?

DUMA   Darkness is not permitted on Death Row.

Night times should be time to avoid humiliation and pain.

Time to use the toilet without someone watching from the door.

Time to eat the supper you were not ready for at three o'clock.

Time to read without being watched or laughed at.
Because reading a book is not reading a book.
It is a conversation, an argument… A love affair with every character. I can't help it. I start talking to myself.

(*YOUNG DUMA, smoking and reading, suddenly talks wildly – as if in conversation with the book.*)

YOUNG DUMA   Kuphelele! Kuphelile!
[It's over! Finished!]

DUMA   Being watched when you are not aware is the most painful thing. It's a constant humiliation. Someone somewhere is watching you all the time.

YOUNG DUMA   (*Talking to the book.*) Awuboni na? [Can't you see it?]

(*DUMA laughs darkly at YOUNG DUMA.*

Screams through the bars, in rage at being spied on.)

Fok off – injas! [Fuck off you dogs!] Dogs!

(*Both DUMA and YOUNG DUMA simultaneously light cigarettes.*)

DUMA   So I smoke to hide. I smoke to survive.

I smoke and wait for morning to come.

WOMAN   And all around you – you hear through the night…

DUMA   The sounds of healthy young men waiting to die.
        Everyone is dreaming – everyone is trying to find their
        way home.
        Some are crying in their sleep. Some are talking.
        Some dream that they are eating, swallowing – because
        the meals here are never enough. Right down the
        corridor, you hear the sound of teeth grinding until the
        morning comes.
        Let me tell you how strong my wife Mandozi is.
        Since my release she has listened to me chewing my
        teeth beside her every night.

WOMAN   You still do it? Even as a free man? After all these years?

DUMA   (*Smiling.*) I have never really come home.
        One thing is certain that I didn't know.
        Every night, I am back there.
        Every night – I go home to Death Row.

        (*He hands her the prisoner's suitcase he was carrying when
        he first entered the performance space.*)

WOMAN   (*Seated, smoking and looking at the untouched suitcase.*)

        He gave me this suitcase. Said I should take it home
        with me. Sometimes we choose to walk away and
        sometimes we open what would be easier to keep
        closed. I was afraid of the things I would learn if I
        opened it… But if I didn't…of things about this
        country I would never know.

        (*She crawls to the suitcase and opens it. Both DUMA and
        YOUNG DUMA take a drag on their cigarettes – and exhale
        a cloud of smoke.*)

        Filled with letters to his girlfriend Mandozi. To his
        brother. His family.

Pages and pages of letters – unsent from Death Row.

(*She looks down at the page she has picked up.*)

5

YOUNG DUMA   Mandozi…

Time passes here in ways you cannot imagine.

DUMA   I have been on Death Row now for almost a week. I have pimples on my face from the stress. I don't have my usual soap. I went to the prison doctor asking for help.

He told me:

WOMAN   This is not a beauty contest.

You are here to die.

(*She turns the page.*)

DUMA   We have to be silent here. Talking is not permitted.

But if I keep my mouth shut all day – it starts to stink.

I have started talking to myself.

(*YOUNG DUMA talks to himself frantically – without sense.*)

The guards here are spies. The only way we can have a private conversation is to use the toilets in our cells.

Soak out the water…

WOMAN   And a toilet becomes a telephone.

(*DUMA and YOUNG DUMA kneel before two different toilets and whisper into the echoing empty bowls.*)

DUMA Through the bowels of Pretoria Maximum Security Prison – the secrets and shit of dying men flow.

(*YOUNG DUMA opens a newspaper. There are holes remaining where articles have been cut out.*)

YOUNG DUMA Our newspapers are censored too.

Anything about the Sharpeville Six is cut away with scissors.

DUMA But the case gives us a kind of dignity. We are the Sharpeville Six.

(*The WOMAN picks up another page.*)

WOMAN Our bodies are now State Property. For this reason we are not permitted to kill ourselves. Our lives are only theirs to take.

DUMA There are no nails in our shoes, or laces… or belts to hang ourselves with. But two men here made a plan.

One stabbed his wrists with a pen.

The other spread soap all over the floor. He tied his neck to the bars on his door. He slipped and ran all the way to his death.

WOMAN Slipped and ran to his death. November '86.

(*She turns the page.*)

YOUNG DUMA This is a factory of death. A living graveyard.

But we find humour here, Mandozi – to normalise the situation…

Forgive us. We laugh at terrible things.

DUMA   There is a boy here – Zakes – who they will hang next week. They interrupted his lunch to take him to the 'Pot' [waiting cells before execution]. He got such a fright – he left his four slices of bread behind.

YOUNG DUMA   Hey Zakes! (*Whistling and calling down the corridor.*)

If you're not going to eat them…

Gee vir my daai vier slie!
[Give me those four slices!]

(*YOUNG DUMA begins to laugh. It is not malicious – but it is infectious.*)

DUMA   We laughed for hours. We laugh at terrible things.

(*DUMA and YOUNG DUMA laugh together.*)

Terminator is the biggest man on Death Row…a giant! But in his sleep we all hear him at night…dreaming he is being hanged…he cries and squeals like a little girl.

(*YOUNG DUMA laughs harder.*)

Then there is Lefty who arrived from the outside world unshaved.

Mandozi…not only did he have a full head of hair… but worse…

YOUNG DUMA   (*Barely able to speak.*) A perm!

He ran past the cells panicking when he got here. We heard him shouting and through the bars, as he passed, we saw his oiled curls.

(*They whistle and cat-call wildly to Lefty. YOUNG DUMA laughs, while DUMA sobers, drags on his cigarette and watches his younger self.*)

DUMA   We laugh here. It helps us to survive.

But do you get that chance…? You – my loved ones at home.

Since this began – we are all of us…on Death Row.

(*YOUNG DUMA's laughter has turned to pain. He sits with his face buried in his hands, and his back against his cell wall. DUMA takes a deep breath and sighs.*)

WOMAN   (*Reading from a document, smoking.*)

'When passing the Death Sentence on the Sharpeville Six, Chief Justice Human admitted, "None of the accused here is directly responsible for the murder, but all are guilty by the Law of Common Purpose."

'An appropriate legal doctrine in its original form, Common Purpose enables a judicial system to convict a person of murder without that person directly causing the victim's death. It is based on a chain of causality. If a murder was a foreseeable result of the accused actions – then the accused is not merely an accessory to the murder – but a perpetrator. In Apartheid South Africa's courts, however, the doctrine was abused. The net of liability was spread to anyone selected as present at the scene of a murder.'

(*To* DUMA, *she grappling to understand.*) So if a crime is based on a chain of causality – how far can you stretch liability? Where does it end?

DUMA   (*Smiles.*) I don't know.

WOMAN   You were not even at the scene of the crime. Why you?

Why you?

DUMA   If not me…who?

(*They stare at each other – as the sound of Miriam Makeba filters over the sound system – as though coming from the tinny speakers in the ceiling of every cell.* YOUNG DUMA *rises, face turned upwards in reverence.*)

YOUNG DUMA   Mandozi, there are speakers in our cells.

Yesterday at twelve forty-five – a thing of dark and terrible beauty happened here. Miriam Makeba – although she is banned – was suddenly playing on the radio. Every man was crying quietly in his cell…

Remembering what it was to have once been alive.

DUMA   It reminded me of Christmas last year. You in that red dress. Your smell, your smile. I was a man – in my own shoes.

YOUNG DUMA   Please keep them safe – my Church Shoes!

Maybe I'll walk in them again some day…

Who knows!

(*He stares through the cage of his cell.* YOUNG DUMA *stands at his cell door with eyes closed. The rumbling sound of men praying in unison is heard. This effect was created*

with a recording of DUMA *reciting The Lord's Prayer,
layered multiple times over itself, until dozens of voices
– all* DUMA's *– fill the air. The sonic effect is haunting and
overwhelming.)*

VOICES Bawo wethu osezulwini, Maliphathwe ngobungcwele
igama lakho.

[Our Father who art in heaven, Hallowed be thy name.]

Ubukumkani bakho mabufike, Intando yakho
mayenziwe emhlabeni, Njengoba isenziwa ezulwini

[Thy kingdom come, Thy will be done, on earth as it is in heaven.]

DUMA For the four hours we are permitted to talk each
day – we dedicate the first hour to prayer…

(The prayer in unison resumes, with YOUNG DUMA *praying
fervently at his cell door.)*

VOICES Siphe namhlanje isonka sethu semihla ngamihla.
Usixolele izono zethu, njengoba nathi sibaxolela abo
basonayo thina.

[Give us this day our daily bread. Forgive us our trespasses, as we
forgive those who trespass against us.]

Ungasingenisi ebuhendweni, usisindise enkohlakalweni.

[Lead us not into temptation, but deliver us from evil.]

Ngokuba ubukumkani bobakho, Namandla ngawakho,
nobungcwalisa bobakho

[For thine is the Kingdom, The power and the glory.]

Kude kube ngunaphakade. Amen.

[Forever and ever. Amen.]

YOUNG DUMA Amen.

WOMAN But immediately after praying, it's chaos – everyone
fights to be heard.

(*YOUNG DUMA shouts down the corridor, competing with a multitude of voices.*)

DUMA   On Tuesday, Peter – the 'Coloured' two cells down – insulted me.

(*As PETER.*) Hey Duma! Hey jou [you] Kaffir [derogatory term used when insulting a black person] – shut die fok op! [the fuck up!]

I have been called 'kaffir' so many times before. But not now!

Not by another man also condemned to die. I did not move for hours. I just stood by my door and waited for morning.

(*YOUNG DUMA stands in stony silence.*)

At seven am they came to take me for a shower.

On my way to the bathrooms, Peter was coming back.

(*Suddenly YOUNG DUMA lashes out violently – as though brutally beating another man. DUMA grabs him from behind and restrains him by holding his arms behind his back.*)

YOUNG DUMA   (*In rage – straining to break free.*)
Daar's jou fokken' KAFFIR! [There's your fuckin' KAFFIR!]

(*Both DUMAS stand side-on, with faces to the audience.*)

DUMA   Peter was hanged the following week. I can still feel his face on my fists. His blood on my hands.

(*YOUNG DUMA looks at his hands.*)

Mandozi – we never reconciled.

(*YOUNG DUMA covers his face with his hands in shame.*)

WOMAN   (*Smoking and reading from a document.*)

'The white regime in SA had the distinction of be̲_̲ one of the bloodiest in history, boasting one of the highest execution rates in the world. Between 1910 and 1989 more than four and a half thousand people were hanged. Approximately half of those were put to death during the 80s – at the height of the anti-Apartheid struggle. It is no coincidence that under the Apartheid government, over 97 percent of the men who went through the trap door were black. As an example of such racial disparity…

'In the period June 1982 – June 1983:

'Of 81 blacks convicted of murdering whites, 38 were executed.

'Of the 52 whites convicted of murdering whites – one was hanged.

'Of the 21 whites convicted of murdering blacks during this period… None were hanged.'*

(*She turns away smoking, continuing to read.*

DUMA and YOUNG DUMA are on their knees. They are scrubbing the floor rhythmically. They are singing together as they work.)

There are volunteers among us who clean Death Row's floors for an extra slice of bread. They also wash the blood and vomit off the hoods used in the hangings each week.

DUMA   Hoods they too will bleed and vomit in as they die. They wash them in the showers – just for extra bread.

---

* *The Death Penalty in South Africa,* Graeme Simpson & Lloyd Vogelman; Centre for the Study of Violence and Reconciliation

WOMAN   (*In uncomprehending horror.*) …Christ…

(*A dark and ominous sound rises. Gates are being opened and shut.*)

DUMA   Mondays, Wednesdays and Fridays.

They stand at the end of the corridor.

(*In the voice of the Prison Wardens.*)

STAAN OP! [Stand up!]

Three times a week – they call out the numbers of those selected to die the following week.

(*YOUNG DUMA stands – as though to military attention. His face is blank but his eyes emanate the terror of this three times weekly Death Selection.*)

(*Shouted brutally.*) V685 V5467 V3214

We hear cells being unlocked and the condemned ordered to pack. Minutes later – these men are gone.

We shout after them as they are taken to the Pot…

YOUNG DUMA   (*Shouting after them.*)
Hamba Kahle Umkhonto. [Go well Soldiers!]

Those who survive – will tell the world!

DUMA   And no matter how hard you try to forget – the Warders will always remind you:

'En jy! Jou dag sal ook kom!'
[And you! Your day will also come!]

YOUNG DUMA   (*In despair.*)
FOKOFF!
[FUCK OFF!]

(He turns away and sinks to the floor of his cell. DUMA takes his seat again and smokes.)

6

WOMAN   *(Reading from a book.)* The Heart Surgeon Professor Chris Barnard describes the hanging of a man as follows: *

'Put a rope around a man's neck. Tie the knot next to his ear. Fasten his wrists behind his back. And drop him a distance of just less than two metres. If you haven't botched it by miscalculating, you'll achieve several things at once: The man's spinal chord will rupture at the point where it enters the skull. It may be necessary to drop him again until the neck is broken. From the time of the first drop, it usually takes between 13 and 15 minutes to die. Electro-chemical discharges will send his limbs flailing in a grotesque dance, eyes and tongue will bulge from the facial apertures under the assault of the rope. And his bowels and bladder will simultaneously void themselves to soil the legs and drip onto the floor…unless you are an efficient hangman who has thoughtfully fitted your subject with a nappy or rubber pants.'

(DUMA exhales a cloud of smoke into the air and stares straight ahead.)

(Grabbing fistfuls of pages from the suitcase – she is overwhelmed.)

Week and week of these pages… I am losing myself.

---

* *Country of my Skull* by Antjie Krog (Vintage, 1999) p 301 quotes Paula McBride who read Dr Chris Barnard's description of death by hanging during her testimony at the TRC.

At night – I start dreaming…

Dreaming I am there!

(*She lies down beside* YOUNG DUMA *– creating the impression of the dozens of sleeping men alone in their cells. They turn in unison from side to side.*)

DUMA On Death Row we dream about dying…

(*They change positions as though tormented by their dreams. The* WOMAN *turns towards* YOUNG DUMA *and she is suddenly lying on top of him, facing him. They move sensuously together.* YOUNG DUMA *rolls over – onto her. They grasp each other feverishly.*)

We dream about

Dying

Food

And women

Every night.

Dreams are so cruel.

They rob you of strength.

(*They roll over and the* WOMAN *rolls away.* YOUNG DUMA *sits up with a start. He is awake and suddenly alone. His body aches with need. He turns into a fetal position and cries out in despair.* DUMA *watches him.*)

I thought you had forgotten me Mandozi. It had been so long,

The morning you arrived to visit me – no one had told me you were coming – but my body knew… I woke and found I had wet my bed like a small boy

I bribed one of the guards to let me wear his jacket.

I wanted to look dignified and strong.

(YOUNG DUMA stands, nervously rearranging his clothes.
He puts on the jacket, which is far too small.)

But I am no longer a man.

I hunger –

like a child.

After sixteen months of staying away

– Mandozi –

Where had you been after all this time?

Finally

You

arrived.

(The WOMAN, nervous but with great tenderness, sits down
on the edge of DUMA's chair, with her back to DUMA – facing
the cage and staring in at YOUNG DUMA in the Visitors'
Booth. YOUNG DUMA leans in and whispers to her.)

YOUNG DUMA   (Violently under his breath, through gritted teeth.)

Where have you been mafazi [woman] ? Where have you
been?

(Hissing.) Just where the FUCK have you been?

(She turns her face away and begins to cry. DUMA laughs
quietly in dark recognition.)

DUMA   The suspicion has started – and like a cancer, you can't
stop it once it's begun.

YOUNG DUMA   Don't bother to come here for a dead man anymore!

Don't bother woman! Don't bother!

(*Erupting in rage.*) DON'T EVEN FUCKING BOTHER!

(*She rises and hurriedly leaves. YOUNG DUMA pushes his fist into his mouth with regret. He pulls against the tide of desperation. DUMA nods, smokes and smiles.*)

DUMA   Time passes here in ways you cannot imagine. It's three years now on Death Row. What is the use of time?

(*He stands and comes face to face with YOUNG DUMA.*)

There are no mirrors here – but in the bathroom by the basin – there is a frosted steel plate. I can just see my outline –

fading away…

(*YOUNG DUMA and DUMA lean in towards one another – trying to see their reflected face.*)

I can't see myself getting older.

YOUNG DUMA   (*Panicking.*) Getting older…can't see my eyes.

WOMAN   (*Dropping all the pages – they float to the floor.*) I can't see myself.

(*DUMA scoops up one single sheet and places it in her hands. She looks into his eyes. Then she reads. DUMA watches her, hands in his pockets, and recites.*)

DUMA   Phinda – how are you brother? I have been here for almost two years now.

I read Eli Wiesel's Book *Night* from the trolley of books here on Death Row. He and his brother ran through the forced marches from Auschwitz – keeping each other alive through the night.

(*DUMA shifts his chair to face the cages, as though he is PHINDA – visiting the YOUNG DUMA, who stands inside the booth.*)

Whenever I feel I will die here – your visits get me through another week.

WOMAN And then the day you brought news from home that Khulu – our youngest brother – was dead.

(*YOUNG DUMA buckles at the knees and falls to the floor.*)

Permission to attend the funeral denied.

(*YOUNG DUMA starts to shake with rage. He holds his hands over his ears, trying to contain the force of an imminent breakdown besieging him. He cries out with his hands over his mouth.*)

DUMA (*Watching YOUNG DUMA dispassionately.*)

I needed someone to hold onto. In the cell opposite mine…

Is an ANC activist – still only a teenager – condemned to die. He had never uttered a word to me before this. But the day my brother died –

(*DUMA moves behind YOUNG DUMA's cage. He speaks to him through the 'bars' – enacting and remembering the words of LUCKY PAYI.*)

(*As LUCKY.*) Mfowetu brother Duma – are you there?

YOUNG DUMA U mang? Who is that?

DUMA (*Whispering.*) It's me brother. Lucky Payi.

(*YOUNG DUMA is silent. He cannot speak.*)

(*Whispering, as* LUCKY PAYI.)
Tell me Bra Duma… [addressed with term of respect by a younger man]

What did you want to say at the graveside to your brother? If they had let you go?

(*YOUNG DUMA is too emotional to speak.* LUCKY PAYI *waits patiently, with a pencil and paper in his hand.*)

YOUNG DUMA (*Finally, struggling to speak.*) Labo ababulala imizimba yethu, abanamandla wokubulala imiphefumulo yethu – [That those who kill our bodies, do not have the power to kill our souls –]

Zange ngathola thuba lokukutshela izinto eziningi Khulu… [I never had a chance to tell you so many things Khulu.]

Zange ngikutshele ukuthi wawusenalo ikusasa…hayi njengami... [That you still had a future…not like me.]

Ngiyaxolisa ukuthi angikwazanga ukukuvelela. [I am sorry I have not been there for you.]

Umama wethu akasekho emhlabeni, futhi ngiyazi ukuthi ubudinga ukuthi ngikuhole kodwa angikwazanga. [We don't have our mother and I know you needed guidance from me - but I couldn't be there.]

Lala ngoxolo nomama wethu Khulu…. [Lie peacefully with our mother Khulu.]

Ngiyeza lapho nikhona Ngizonibona nobabili kwelizayo

[I am coming there where you are. I will see you both soon, on the other side.]

Imina umfowenu – Duma Joshua Kumalo

[It's me – your brother – Duma Joshua Kumalo.]

ALL   V 34-58.

DUMA   That summer – Lucky read me a book late at night, across the corridor, through the bars of his cell door.

WOMAN   (*Reading a passage from* View from Coyaba.]

'To live with the conscious knowledge of the shadow of uncertainty, with the knowledge that disaster or tragedy could strike at any time; to be afraid and to know and acknowledge your fear, and still to live creatively and with unstinting love: that is to live with grace.'

DUMA: *View from Coyaba* by Peter Abrahms. Lucky Payi was a young ANC Cadre condemned to die. He was an orphan with no family. I never saw him have a visitor, not one letter ever came for him. But that child of Death Row taught me how to face dying.

YOUNG DUMA   'We do not go in vain. Our blood will nourish the tree of freedom.'

Hey Lucky? Read page 24 again, Bru [Brother].

DUMA   Mfowetu, Brother, try to sleep. We have time.

But they called Lucky's number that Tuesday morning.

WOMAN   V 89-76.

YOUNG DUMA (*Grasping the cage door with despair.*) No!

DUMA For four hours that night, the whole section sang for him.

(*DUMA and YOUNG DUMA stand to attention and sing. YOUNG DUMA is crying as he sings. DUMA watches his younger self grieve.*)

BOTH DUMAS Hamba Kahle Umkhonto*
[Go well Soldier / Spear]
We mkhonto
[Soldier / Spear]
Mkhonto We Sizwe
[Soldier / Spear of the Nation.]

DUMA But at eight pm, every night on Death Row – silence had to fall.

Everything I had said in my cell the morning my brother died – Lucky had written down and posted it to my family, asking them to read it at Khulu's graveside. Lucky Payi – orphan of the world – child of Death Row. Who had never been with a woman – still a child. You taught me – even in that place – how to be free.

YOUNG DUMA (*Breaking the silence with a whisper, searching for the words.*)

Lucky…mfowetu… [my brother…]

Hamba grand [Go well] tomorrow. Be strong.

I will see you on the other side…

* A song of defiance against the Apartheid regime, sung for fallen heroes of the political struggle. It was sung by the men on Death Row (often through the night) as a salute to those about to be executed.

YAEL FARBER & DUMA KUMALO

(*But there is silence from LUCKY's cell.*)

DUMA   There were no more words.

I woke at dawn when they opened Lucky's door.

(*YOUNG DUMA sits bolt upright at the sound of LUCKY's door being unlocked.*)

He left quietly.

That's all.

7

(*DUMA turns away and sits in his chair. YOUNG DUMA stands pressed against his cage – his eyes cast down. Something has shifted in him. There is focused preparation for death – a quality in YOUNG DUMA that has gone beyond bearable pain. Music from far away underscores the following. It is a dark note – a drone – that suggests a point of no return.*)

DUMA   The Dead live with us here. We wear their clothes, their shoes,
We sleep under blankets that still have their smell.
We eat from plastic plates with plastic spoons that break because the porridge is too heavy. Everything is disposable.

Jomo
Fofo
Lefty
Gaza
Shepard
Koos…

I watch them come and go.

BOTH DUMAS   (*Like an incantation – recited together.*)

V6578
V8769
V6521
V8734
V3215

(*The distorted sound of a Christmas Carol is heard from far away. YOUNG DUMA takes some tinsel decorations and pushes them into the grid of his caged cell.*)

DUMA   Happy Christmas Mandozi.

I dream I am home.

Here the rate of execution has increased.

Last week they hanged 21 men in a single morning. They had to reach their quota of annual executions before they closed for the Festive Season. They had to wash away the blood on the steps with buckets. They throw sweets in our cells. They have decorated Death Row with Christmas colours and balloons.

(*The sound of Nina Simone's 'Young, Gifted and Black' slowly overwhelms the sound of the dark Christmas Carol. YOUNG DUMA is lost in memory.*)

YOUNG DUMA   Hey, Mandozi! Remember the night we made love.

Nina Simone was playing. The mattress was too big for the base. Shit! We didn't notice until it was too late and we fell on our arses on the floor…laughed so much… couldn't stop…laughed and laughed.

(*YOUNG DUMA laughs until he is in tears.*)

Pray for me, Mandozi. Maybe – someday – soon…

(The WOMAN looks up from the letters to see the YOUNG DUMA returning home. For a moment she is Mandozi. She drops the page which floats to the floor. YOUNG DUMA takes her strongly in his arms. Their shadow is cast on the back wall as they dance gently together to the song. Lights fade as DUMA watches silently from his chair. The song plays out in the dark.

A lamp flickers on. The WOMAN is alone – surrounded by the pages she dropped earlier.)

WOMAN   Tried to file the letters. But how do you arrange the un-arrangeable? Order what is shattered? Name what cannot be said? Mostly we sit in silence – in the eye of the storm – where it's quiet… But in that unnamable silence we have to try…or the truth will never come home. Guilty by common purpose.

But in the ever-widening circle of responsibility – where does liability end? Who – by this law of common purpose – would be responsible for the death of that town councillor on a dusty Sharpeville Street? From an enraged mob; to those who enforced impossible laws; to the designers of a constitution that unleashed a million consequences…where does liability end? And what of us – the bystanders: participating by apathy in a crime against humanity. By the notion of Common Purpose we all conspired in that man's death. Every day I hear people pleading extenuating circumstances here.

'We were just living our lives. We didn't know.'

Where had I heard those words before? We saw the smoke and the ovens, but we didn't know. If I have my father's eyes…what have I seen? How is it that we forget?

(The sound of the protest song 'Siyaya ePitoli' begins to grow. It is a slow, dark version of this usually triumphant, upbeat and defiant song.)

Siyaya ePitoli! *

[We are going to Pretoria!]

Siyaya ePitoli!

[We are going to Pretoria!]

Siyaya ePitoli!

[We are going to Pretoria!]

Siyaya! Siyaya!

[We are going! We are going!]

(Lights shift as the song fills the auditorium. YOUNG DUMA and the WOMAN fade to silhouettes and DUMA stands. He takes his last drag on a cigarette and crushes it beneath his foot on the floor.)

8

(With hands in his pockets, the neon above him flickers on. He looks up simply at the audience in this naked light.)

DUMA   I am Duma Joshua Kumalo.

In 1984 I was condemned to death for a crime I did not commit. I spent three years on Death Row waiting to die.

On December 13 1988 –

My number was called.

---

* A song of protest sung at mass action rallies and refers to marching to The Houses of Parliament in Pretoria – seat of the Apartheid Government during its reign.

(*He is quiet for some time. He simply looks at the audience.*)

(*Finally.*) There are no words to describe this moment.

To explain what it's like to leave your body behind.

(*DUMA turns to watch the YOUNG DUMA argue for extra time. DUMA stands close, but is calm and detached.*)

YOUNG DUMA   (*Still reeling, grasping.*) We are supposed to have seven day's notice.

December 18th gives us only five.

WOMAN   You are welcome to write a letter to the Chief Justice and lodge a complaint.

DUMA   We knew they were hurrying our executions before the world could know and protest.

YOUNG DUMA   (*Laughing bitterly.*) They will find us cold before they get our complaint! The post takes a week.

WOMAN   We are a prison not a post office! You can take it up with them.

Trek uit! [Strip!]

(*Without options, YOUNG DUMA strips.*)

DUMA   We sit naked on a bench waiting. I tell the others with me: 'Magents, Guys, I am shaking – but I am not afraid.'

(*The WOMAN hands DUMA a tape measure. YOUNG DUMA stands on DUMA's chair.*)

DUMA   We who are about to be hanged on South Africa's
        Death Row

        Must be weighed and measured.

        (*DUMA wraps the tape measure around* YOUNG DUMA's
        throat.)

        For the size of the noose.

WOMAN   Neck: 28 centimetres.

        (*DUMA runs the tape measure down the length of* YOUNG
        DUMA's *body.*)

        Two metres.

DUMA   And our coffin's length.

        (*Turning to the audience.*)
        When does the soul leave the body?

        Tell me: How many times can a man die?

        (*As* YOUNG DUMA *gathers his clothes to dress.*)

WOMAN   Get dressed – maar los hulle! [– but leave them!]

        Your underpants, shoes and socks… You will have no
        need of such things anymore. You are dead men now.
        Leave these things on the floor.

DUMA   We are each given R7 pocket money to spend at the
        prison shop on sweets or tobacco. We will each get
        a boiled, deboned chicken the night before we are
        hanged. These are the things a man's life comes to on
        South Africa's Death Row…

        And then…we are sent to the Pot.

        We have five days in which we must prepare to die.

(The sound of men praying in unison builds and reverberates through the system. Desperate weeping and laughter is drowned out by a dark and doomed version of 'Ave Maria'. YOUNG DUMA kneels at DUMA's feet. DUMA feeds him the wafer of his last sacrament. He swallows the wafer and stands. DUMA and the WOMAN reconfigure the cages tightly around YOUNG DUMA. He stands in shadows in the centre of the Pot. He runs his hands over his torso and into his pants. He masturbates. He puts his head back and cries out with his life force – but any vocalization disappears into the noises of the Pot. YOUNG DUMA disappears into the dark.)

DUMA   *(Asking the audience.)* How many times can a man die?

(The WOMAN helps DUMA into a jacket. On him it is too small and has the effect of creating the image of a humble and broken man – come to say goodbye to his son. YOUNG DUMA steps into the visitor's booth. He is a hollow version of the young man we have seen through this journey. He is exhausted and broken. He faces his father through the cage. He cannot look him in the eyes.)

DUMA   When my father paid his final visit, he requested only one thing: to know where he could collect my bones after the hanging – to give his son a proper burial. I had to explain that I was State Property. That nothing of his son's remains would belong to him again.

(YOUNG DUMA weeps as his father speaks quietly to him in Zulu. As DUMA and YOUNG DUMA enact this final farewell, the WOMAN turns to the audience.)

WOMAN   The case of the Sharpeville Six (as Duma and his co-accused became known) captured the attention of the world. Despite the South African Government's hurried attempt to secretly hang the condemned before word broke – this information was leaked across the globe.

(*DUMA turns to listen to her, leaving YOUNG DUMA in this moment of the past, alone.*)

DUMA   Fifteen hours before being hanged – news of the hanging reached the world. Under intense international pressure – the state reluctantly granted Duma and his five co-accused a temporary stay of execution.

WOMAN   To come back after you have already said your goodbyes…

DUMA   Fuck them!

We were already dead inside.

The Warders pushed us back to our cells.

(*DUMA pushes YOUNG DUMA back to his cell. There is a full boiled chicken in a plate on the floor and a stack of letters in envelopes.*)

All the goodbye letters to my family had been placed on my bed unsent. This was the Warders' final cruelty to me. They had wanted me to go to my death knowing the letters would never be sent.

(*YOUNG DUMA rips the letters apart in rage, and throws the fragments upwards. They shower down on him.*)

In the corner was my last meal – a deboned chicken – waiting for me. The had brought it to my cell before they knew of our temporary reprieve.

WOMAN   What did you do?

DUMA   (*He laughs wildly.*) I ate that fuckin'chicken…

Before that chicken could eat me!

(*YOUNG DUMA, with a mouth full of chicken, laughs in rage and defiance. DUMA picks up the WOMAN, spins her until her feet are off the ground. DUMA breaks from her and goes over to the cage to watch YOUNG DUMA eat.*)

WOMAN   It would be a further four years of serving a life sentence in prison before Duma Joshua Kumalo V 34-58 would be free to go home – released along with hundreds of other prisoners as part of political negotiations.

9

(*The WOMAN and DUMA hold the cages on both side and open them outwards from top end. YOUNG DUMA steps forward into the world. His protracted walk brings him centre stage. At his feet is the shoe box with his Church Shoes untouched inside. He takes them out of the box, and, overcome with emotion – he bows his head and quietly weeps.*)

DUMA   (*Watching YOUNG DUMA.*) Coming home was the hardest thing of all. I was a stranger with my loved ones. This was no longer my home.

WOMAN   We know nothing – bitching about the new Constitution. The pain! We don't have a clue.

DUMA   Pain is pain baby. Pain is where we all eventually will land.

(*YOUNG DUMA, wrapped in a grey blanket, sits resolutely with a stony face. DUMA circles him.*)

My name had not been cleared. I was still a murderer in the eyes of the law. I went to Sharpeville Police Station for a sit-in and hunger strike!

WOMAN   For sixteen days, he refused to leave the station or eat – until they reopened his case and cleared his name. Finally he went to Pretoria, to see the Chief Magistrate. He boarded a train and arrived wrapped in his blanket – straight from Sharpeville Police Station.

YOUNG DUMA   (*Stony-faced with a command borne of despair.*)
I am Duma Joshua Kumalo. V3458.

(*Holding a large, leather-bound book, DUMA enacts the dismissive Chief Magistrate.*)

DUMA   My boy, I know all about you. Look here. You were found guilty by a Court of Law. It says so here in this book. Ask your Mandela for your name to be cleared. Don't come here again and waste my time.

(*YOUNG DUMA steps back. He has been pushed beyond the point of return by these callous words.*)

I waited until after Christmas. I packed a bag with some books – knowing I would be jailed again after what I planned to do…

Then I went back to that court with an axe.

YOUNG DUMA   Ke ne ke dubehile ka hare. [I could no longer contain the pain inside.]

(*YOUNG DUMA – with an axe over his shoulder – walks in circles around DUMA with growing rage and focused intensity. His whole journey on Death Row has been leading to this point of anger and pain.*)

DUMA   I could no longer hold the chaos. It was starting
        to erupt inside! My father – now an old man…
        SHATTERED! Phinda! [SHATTERED!]

My sister's life and marriage SHATTERED!

Khulu DEAD.

My family.

My life.

My everything.

SHATTERED!

Seven years that had robbed us of everything – and he
told me NOT TO WASTE HIS FUCKEN' TIME! (*Explosive.*)

(*YOUNG DUMA starts to swing the axe. DUMA steps behind
him, swiftly taking the axe away. YOUNG DUMA's motions
continue, but in this move, he has exchanged the axe for
the green death row uniforms in his hands. He swings these
around his head – creating a blur of movement expressing
his erupting anger, destruction and pain. He builds in
intensity until he is out of control.*)

DUMA   I destroyed everything in that empty courtroom with
        my axe.

(*When the intensity of this action has peaked, YOUNG
DUMA drops to his knees and pushes the axe away from
himself in surrender, and rolls into a fetal position on the
floor with his hands over his ear, weeping. DUMA moves
towards his younger self. He is on his knees. He takes the
YOUNG DUMA and holds him. DUMA closes his eyes and sits
quietly, rocking YOUNG DUMA – holding the past.*)

10

WOMAN   Case Number 861 of the Truth and Reconciliation Commission for Human Rights Violations. I met him after a question and answer session in Sebokeng '96 – on a dry autumn day.

What do we do after such knowledge? I had asked… We tell stories – he told me. We find the words for what can never be described.

DUMA   This is our history. We all come from this broken place. Either you are in or you are out. But if you choose to be in – you must partake.

(*He hands her the cloth from a basin of water and together they clean YOUNG DUMA from head to toe. DUMA sings as this ritual is performed.*)

Hamba Kahle Umkhonto

[Go well Soldier / Spear]

We mkhonto

[Soldier / Spear]

Mkhonto We Sizwe

[Soldier / Spear of the Nation.]

(*YOUNG DUMA stands and slowly moves to the shadows of the back wall.*)

WOMAN   Pretoria Maximum Security Prison still stands its ground today – though the gallows have been closed.

We visited it together the last time I saw him – before he walked away.

(*They stand beside each other.*)

Climbing the fifty-two steps to the gallows, he suddenly smiled…

You OK?

DUMA   (*He winks.*) Sharp babela! [Fine baby!] This time, I know I'll be coming down.

WOMAN   The trap door now stands silent – boarded up and covered with cement. The centre of the roof above it is sagging from the weight of all those executed men. For a long time – we were the busiest gallows in the world.

The shoes we found in a dusty store room behind the uniforms…

DUMA   Worn by the forgotten men of Death Row.

We could – any of us – have walked in these shoes.

(*The WOMAN goes to the pile of shoes. DUMA brings audience members onto the stage to help in the process of finding the matching partner for each shoe, and laying the pairs out in a long line across the stage. DUMA holds a calabash of water and walks along the line of shoes, sprinkling water on them. He recites his praise names as an incantation. He speaks to the ancestors – asking for their presence in this ritual.*

Once the audience members have returned to their seats – DUMA considers the line of 21 pairs of shoes.)

A single morning's killings at Christmas time 1987, on South Africa's Death Row.

(*The WOMAN looks back over her shoulder at YOUNG DUMA against the back wall, smoking. They hold one another's gaze and then YOUNG DUMA turns and moves into the shadows.*)

(*Whispers to the WOMAN.*) Let's go.

(*They walk away; leaving the YOUNG DUMA in his grey blanket, smoking and pacing along the walls in the dark.*)

11

(*Golden light grows on DUMA and the WOMAN as they turn away.*)

WOMAN   Outside, the light is beautiful – a typical day in down town Pretoria. Beautiful old Jacaranda trees lining the streets. Purple carpets of flowers that – after Highveld thunderstorms – popped beneath my childhood feet.

(*The WOMAN hands DUMA the manuscript.*)

DUMA   (*He nods and tucks the story under his arm.*)
If not me – who?

(*He hands her a box.*)

WOMAN   What is it?

(*She opens it. Inside are his untouched Church Shoes.*)

Your Church Shoes? Still brand new. Why don't you want them?

DUMA   I wore them during my trial, dreamed of them as I prepared to die in my bare feet. All that mattered was that they kept them for me in case I came home. But I am no longer the man who once walked in those shoes. Give them to someone who has miles to go!

(*He smiles and touches her cheek.*)

                     YAEL FARBER & DUMA KUMALO

We have our fathers' eyes. Remember what we have seen. That we may never forget.

WOMAN   (*Turning to the audience.*) ...And I know I am home. For better or worse – we call this broken place 'home'.

(*She moves away and out of the performance space, back into the auditorium.*)

EPILOGUE

(DUMA sits in his chair as at the start of the play. He looks at the audience. He waits. After some time, he nods and speaks.)

DUMA   Exactly a year to the day I was supposed to be hanged

On the 18th of December, my son Jorgi was born.

A day that was cursed with my death – became a blessing of new life.

And I …

I live on borrowed time….

Telling my story to those willing to listen. I speak for the dead.

For we who survived must tell the world.

Outside, a new day is beginning in Pretoria, South Africa.

And I am here to see it.

I – Duma Joshua Kumalo

Prisoner V 34-58.

(Lights fade until he is a silhouette in his chair, smoking. He stands, looks at the performance area and nods. He walks to the door he entered from – opening the door and letting light stream into the venue from outside. He walks out of the door, leaving it open and the audience with themselves.)

(Ends.)

YAEL FARBER & DUMA KUMALO